Standards-Based
Assessment Resource

Grade 6

Houghton
Mifflin
Harcourt

Contents

Overview

Assessments and Performance Tasks

As you use the Houghton Mifflin Harcourt *Journeys* instructional program, you have a rich array of materials to foster students' achievement week by week and unit by unit. The *Standards-Based Assessment Resource* includes Assessments and Performance Tasks that align with the content in *Journeys* and give students practice with the high-stakes tests they will encounter. Rigorous tasks and questions, complex text, and technology-enhanced item formats (online only) prepare students for success on standards-based assessments. At the end of each unit, you can use an Assessment or Performance Task to obtain a broader picture of achievement.

Assessments

The Assessments can be given three times per year, at the end of Units 1, 3, and 5. These tests are cumulative. The Unit 1 Assessment draws from Unit 1, while the Units 3 and 5 Assessments draw upon skills that have been taught in the current and previous units. The item types and assessment formats presented are the same kinds that students will encounter on high-stakes tests and provide essential practice in test-taking strategies.

Each Assessment has four sections. The Reading section assesses comprehension and vocabulary strategies. The Writing section draws upon the grammar, spelling, and writing skills taught to date. The Listening section presents audio or read-aloud passages that assess the listening skills that students will encounter on high-stakes tests. The Research section assesses a combination of comprehension, research/media literacy, and writing skills.

The Listening section of the Assessments includes a source that students must listen to and then answer questions about. The source will not be available as text to students. If you administer a paper-and-pencil version of the Assessments, you will read the source aloud to students. If you administer the online Assessment, students will need to access audio on a computer.

Performance Tasks

The Performance Tasks can also be given three times per year, at the end of Units 2, 4, and 6. Each Performance Task draws upon the reading, writing, and research skills taught in the current and previous units. These tasks encourage students to integrate knowledge and skills to conduct complex analysis and research.

A brief Classroom Activity will be conducted prior to each Performance Task to orient students to the context of the task. The Classroom Activity includes a summary of one source from the Performance Task and prompts for a classroom discussion. At the end of the Classroom Activity, the teacher will be directed to make a brief statement that explains the purpose of the activity within the context of the Performance Task as a whole.

Each Performance Task features two parts. Part 1 introduces a group of related text sources. Students should be encouraged to take notes as they read the sources. After the sources, students will encounter a set of questions related to the passage. The answers to the items will be scored. Part 2 introduces the essay prompt, along with a brief description of the scoring criteria. The essay will be scored using one of three rubrics.

General Guidelines for Administering

The Assessments and Performance Tasks are group-administered and may be taken online or as a paper-and-pencil version. At Kindergarten and Grade 1, some sections of the tests are read aloud. These sections are noted in the specific guidelines for administering the tests. At Grade 2 and beyond, students can read the directions and take the tests independently. At all grades, the Listening section of the Assessments and the Classroom Activity of the Performance Tasks will be administered by the teacher.

Test Time

The Assessments are not timed. The Performance Tasks have suggested completion times listed on the teacher overview pages.

Allowable Resources

Students may access several resources while they complete the Assessments and Performance Tasks.

Pen/pencil/highlighter and blank/lined paper: Students are encouraged to take notes throughout the Performance Tasks, and they may choose to take notes as they complete the Assessments.

Hard-copy dictionary: Students are allowed to access dictionaries as they write the essay during Part 2 of the Performance Task.

Headphones: All students will need headphones to complete the Listening section of each online Assessment.

Item Types

The Assessments and the Performance Tasks include the following item types:

- Selected-response items: These multiple-choice items require students to choose an answer from several provided options. Some items will require students to select multiple correct options.

- Constructed-response items: These items require students to write or type a response.

- Interactive items: Interactive items require students to complete a table or underline a portion of the text. Interactive items online require students to interact with the text by clicking cells in a table or highlighting a portion of text.

Guidelines for Administering Assessment 1

Use the following directions as you administer each section.

Reading, Writing, and Research

Students will read the passages and stimuli independently, and then they will complete the corresponding items.

Listening

The Listening prompts are below for read-aloud presentation.

Say: *Listen to the presentation. Then answer the questions about the presentation.*

The Great Thinker

Isaac Newton was born in England in 1642. As a child, he was always thinking about experiments he wanted to perform. As a teen, he created several types of kites. He tested and tried to improve each kite in order to determine which shape flew the best. In 1655, he spent a year experimenting. He became the first person to prove that sunlight contains all the colors of the rainbow. He did this by experimenting with a triangular piece of glass called a prism. When a beam of light passes through a prism, the light breaks apart into different colors, forming a rainbow.

But Newton is most famous for his findings about gravity. It is a myth that he had an instant flash of understanding when an apple fell to the ground. However, Newton's observation of a falling apple did start a process of thinking about what kind of force could affect both apples and planets.

Say: *Listen to the presentation. Then answer the questions about the presentation.*

Jackie Robinson—Breaking Barriers

When the National Association of Base Ball Players was formed in 1867, it banned African American players. But on April 15, 1947, a young athlete named Jackie Robinson changed the face of baseball and the United States. On that day, Robinson stepped onto the field in a Brooklyn Dodgers uniform. It was the first attempt to break the unwritten code of the color barrier in baseball.

Robinson had been playing for the Kansas City Monarchs, a team in the Negro American League. Branch Rickey, president and general manager of the Brooklyn Dodgers, saw him play and approached him about playing for the Dodgers. Rickey warned Robinson about what to expect. He told him that he would have to ignore whatever abuse came his way. Robinson knew that his example would help other African American players get a chance to play. Today, Jackie Robinson is remembered as one of America's heroes, having changed our country for the better.

Say: *Listen to the presentation. Then answer the questions about the presentation.*

Saving Our Rivers

Rivers are the lifeblood of a region. They are an important source of drinking water. They also are used for irrigation and the production of energy. These waterways often play a role in a community's economy because of the recreational activities they support. Keeping them clean and safe is a goal everyone should share.

But America's rivers are in trouble. Over half of them are unable to support the fish and vegetation that are important parts of the river ecosystem. Another 23 percent of the rivers have pollution issues that could lead to future problems. Only 21 percent of our rivers are described by the Environmental Protection Agency (EPA) as "healthy biological communities" able to sustain life.

Since the American Rivers organization started the National River Cleanup in 1991, over a million volunteers have eliminated more than twenty million pounds of litter. When river savers roll up their sleeves and get to work, the results can be impressive!

Guidelines for Administering Performance Task 1

The Mystery of the Viking Ship

Classroom Activity *(20 minutes)*

1. Allow students to independently read "The Mystery of the Viking Ship." This article was written to inform readers about an important archaeological find—a Viking ship found on a farm in Norway. The article describes how the structure of the ship helped it move efficiently through the water. It also describes a burial site within the stern of the ship. A skeleton and the items found with the skeleton tell us much about the customs of the Vikings.

2. Lead a brief class discussion about the article, using the questions below.

   Question 1: How was the ship built? What does that tell us about the life of Vikings?

   Question 2: What are some items found in the burial site? What do these tell us about the person who was buried there?

3. Explain that students will use this article and two other articles to write a narrative about the Vikings for other students and teachers.

Student Task Overview

Part 1 *(55 minutes)*

Students will examine the additional stimulus independently and will take notes. They will then respond to constructed-response and selected-response items.

Part 2 *(45 minutes)*

Students will continue to have access to the sources they utilized in the Classroom Activity and Part 1. They will refer to their notes and their answers to the items to write a narrative. They will prewrite, draft, and revise that narrative. The narrative created at the end of Part 2 will be scored. Reading notes in Part 1 and prewriting and drafting in Part 2 will not be scored.

Task Specifications and Scoring Rubrics

Review the REMEMBER section at the end of the student performance task to remind students about the elements of a well-written narrative.

Score student responses using the Performance Task: Narrative Writing Rubric.

Guidelines for Administering Assessment 2

Use the following directions as you administer each section.

Reading, Writing, and Research

Students will read the passages and stimuli independently, and then they will complete the corresponding items.

Listening

The Listening prompts are below for read-aloud presentation.

Say: *Listen to the presentation. Then answer the questions about the presentation.*

Life under the Han Dynasty

The Han dynasty lasted over four centuries. During that time, the lives of farmers and ordinary people improved. Although men still had to serve time in the military or work on government projects, the demands were not as severe as they had been in the past.

The government still made many rules about everyday life. Farmers, who were allowed to remain on their land, rose with the sun and worked until dark. In the winter months, farmers were expected to practice archery so they could protect their home and property against intruders. They were also expected to re-plaster houses and repair storage bins and animal pens. Their wives were to keep busy making sandals and weaving cloth.

Preparing the soil, sowing seeds, irrigating crops, gathering herbs, harvesting grain, and laying in supplies occupied the other seasons. In summer, the women washed old clothes and dyed the silk before taking it to market. The children's job was to watch over the chickens or pigs.

Say: *Listen to the presentation. Then answer the questions about the presentation.*

What Pompeii Can Tell Us

A major step in solving the mysteries of Pompeii began in 1994, when a university initiated a project to explore one block of the ancient Roman city. Students from around the world came to dig and catalog artifacts there. Their work has helped scientists learn more about the ancient Roman world as it was in CE 79 when Mount Vesuvius erupted.

Workers collected evidence with trowels. They used brushes to carefully scrape away the soil. They found traces of a wide range of foods, which provided evidence of what people ate. Then scientists looked at the recipes from a Roman named Apicius. He lived just before the destruction of Pompeii. His recipes were collected centuries after his death and put in an authentic ancient Roman cookbook.

Scientists at Pompeii looked over the list of foods found in the area and matched them to the cookbook. They found many recipes that might have been made in the gourmet kitchen of a wealthy family.

Say: *Listen to the presentation. Then answer the questions about the presentation.*

The Navajos

The Navajos are a Native American group found in the Southwest. They first settled on the Colorado Plateau and formed their own unique culture.

The Navajos were originally nomadic hunters and gatherers. They sometimes raided other settlements, particularly those of the Spanish, but their primary goal was to acquire more livestock. By the end of the 1700s, the Navajos were noted for the size of their flocks and herds and their successful methods of raising animals.

The Navajos lived in clans, placing their hogans together. Hogans were structures framed with poles and then covered with earth. In 1863, the US government forced the Navajos to move to a new settlement in eastern New Mexico. Known as the Long Walk, hundreds died along the way, and thousands died of starvation and disease in the reservation. Four years later, they were allowed to return to a small area in northwestern New Mexico. Today, many Navajos remain on this reservation.

Guidelines for Administering Performance Task 2

The Fight for Civil Rights

Classroom Activity *(20 minutes)*

1. Allow students to independently read "Civil Rights and the Supreme Court." This article was written to inform readers about a Supreme Court decision that ended the segregation of black and white students in schools. The article describes how segregation usually resulted in far inferior conditions for blacks. In 1954, *Brown v. Board of Education* set out to end segregation, specifically in schools. This case paved the way for more equal civil rights for blacks.

2. Lead a brief class discussion about the passage using the questions below.

   Question 1: Why did segregation last as long as it did?

   Question 2: Once integration was in place, how did change occur in the Deep South?

3. Explain that students will use this article and two others to write a report about civil rights in the United States.

Student Task Overview

Part 1 *(55 minutes)*

Students will examine the additional stimulus independently and will take notes. They will then respond to constructed-response and selected-response items.

Part 2 *(45 minutes)*

Students will continue to have access to the sources they used in the Classroom Activity and Part 1. They will refer to their notes and their answers to the items to write an article. They will prewrite, draft, and revise the article. The article created at the end of Part 2 will be scored. Reading notes in Part 1 and prewriting and drafting in Part 2 will not be scored.

Task Specifications and Scoring Rubrics

Review the REMEMBER section at the end of the student performance task to remind students about the elements of a well-written informative article.

Score student responses using the Performance Task: Informative/Explanatory Writing Rubric.

Guidelines for Administering Assessment 3

Use the following directions as you administer each section.

Reading, Writing, and Research

Students will read the passages and stimuli independently, and then they will complete the corresponding items.

Listening

The Listening prompts are below for read-aloud presentation.

Say: *Listen to the presentation. Then answer the questions about the presentation.*

Life on the International Space Station

Life on the International Space Station (ISS) is definitely a departure from life on Earth. The biggest distinction, of course, is that because of the lack of gravity in space, you float everywhere you go. "I didn't sit down for six months on the space station," commented astronaut Sunita "Suni" Williams. Still, many astronauts can play games or read books to keep themselves busy.

When ISS astronauts want some time to themselves, they can escape into private sleeping cabins that are about three times larger than a phone booth, Williams reported. They may be compact, but they contain quite a view—each cabin has a window for gazing out into space! Williams kept books and photos of her family tucked inside her cabin, which made it feel "like your own little house," she said.

Inside her cabin, Williams slept while floating in a sleeping bag attached to the wall. Sleeping in space was more difficult than she had expected—she missed having a pillow to lay her head on.

Say: *Listen to the presentation. Then answer the questions about the presentation.*

What Can We Learn from Archaeology?

The science of archaeology is a doorway from modern times to ancient civilizations. Through precise methods, archaeologists discover artifacts that reveal how people used to live, enabling us to understand much more about ancient cultures.

Once an exploration area is chosen, scientists take a walking tour. Sometimes, they thump the ground and listen—depending on the sound, it can indicate a building or a hole underneath. Sometimes they push long rods into the ground to get an idea of what might be underneath; however, Global Positioning System (GPS) satellites make establishing an exact location much easier.

When the digging commences, workers must proceed very carefully. Scientists want to recover artifacts without breaking or damaging them. When workers discover an object, they catalog its exact location. Excavated objects are then carefully cleaned and studied in a laboratory to determine their age and what they are made of. Then scientists sort and analyze all of the objects to make sense of what they have found.

Say: *Listen to the presentation. Then answer the questions about the presentation.*

The Qin Dynasty

China united for the first time under the Qin dynasty, but this dynasty's rule was harsh and short-lived. Ying Cheng became the king of Qin at age 13. He planned to conquer and unite the seven warring states in China, which he did within 20 years. Ying Cheng became Qin Shi Huang, First Sovereign Emperor of Qin.

Qin Shi Huang imposed an extensive code of laws based on legalist principles, which emphasized the use of force to control the population. Lawbreakers were brutally punished.

Qin Shi Huang wanted his dynasty to last for "10,000 generations," but his family ruled for 15 years. He governed with an iron hand and survived several assassination attempts. After his death in 210 BCE, rebellions broke out. In 202 BCE, after defeating the Qin army, Liu Bang won the throne and became the first ruler of the Han dynasty.

Guidelines for Administering Performance Task 3

Robot Technology

Classroom Activity *(20 minutes)*

1. Allow students to independently read "Human Robots." This article shows the ways that robots have developed humanlike characteristics to more effectively help human beings. The text discusses several groundbreaking achievements in the development of robotics, including a robot that was developed to help with a human weight-loss program.

2. Lead a brief class discussion about the article, using the questions below.

   Question 1: How have robots been developed to fully connect with human beings? How do key details in the article help explain this main idea?

   Question 2: What are some of the ways that robots can be helpful to our society?

3. Explain that students will use this article and two other articles to write an argumentative essay about robots for other students and teachers.

Student Task Overview

Part 1 *(55 minutes)*

Students will examine the additional stimuli independently and will take notes. They will then respond to constructed-response and selected-response items.

Part 2 *(45 minutes)*

Students will continue to have access to the sources they used in the Classroom Activity and Part 1. They will refer to their notes and their answers to the items in Part 1 to write an essay. They will prewrite, draft, and revise that report. The essay created at the end of Part 2 will be scored. Reading notes from Part 1 and prewriting and drafting from Part 2 will not be scored.

Task Specifications and Scoring Rubrics

Review the REMEMBER section at the end of the student performance task to remind students about the elements of a well-written argumentative essay.

Score student responses using the Performance Task: Argument Writing Rubric.

Scoring and Interpreting the Results

Scoring

The answers to the Assessments and Performance Tasks can be found in the Answer Keys section. Each correct response to a selected-response item is worth one point. Each constructed-response item is worth two points. Constructed-response items and essay responses should be scored using the rubrics provided in this book. Sample answers to the constructed-response items are given on the Answer Key and should be used as a guide to score a student's responses. Because these questions require students to think deeply about comprehension, both the teacher and students can learn a great deal by discussing students' responses and their reasoning.

Duplicate a Test Record Form for each student and enter the scores in the Student Score column. This form will allow you to track a student's performance across the year. If you require a percentage score for each test to help in assigning grades, apply the formula in the optional Final Score row and record that score.

Interpreting

Consider each student's scores on the Test Record Form. Students who achieve an Acceptable Score (indicated on the form) or higher are most likely ready to move to the next unit in the book.

For struggling students, duplicate the Answer Key. Circle the item numbers answered incorrectly for each Assessment or Performance Task and compare the corresponding skills indicated. Look for patterns among the errors to help you decide which skills need reteaching and more practice.

Assessment 1

Item Number	Correct Answer	Unit, Lesson, Program Skill	Depth of Knowledge
		READING	
1	ascend	U1L5: Vocabulary Strategy: Reference Sources	2
2	C, D, E	U1L1: Comprehension: Understanding Characters	3
3	B	U1L1: Comprehension: Simile	3
4	A	U1L4: Comprehension: Alliteration	2
5	D	U1L3: Vocabulary Strategy: Multiple-Meaning Words	2
6	A	U1L4: Vocabulary Strategy: Prefixes *de-, trans-*	2
7	A, C, E	U1L4: Comprehension: Story Structure	3
8	B	U1L1: Comprehension: Dialogue	3
9	A	U1L1: Comprehension: Understanding Characters	1
10	A	U1L3: Comprehension: Diagrams	3
11	A	U1L3: Vocabulary Strategy: Multiple-Meaning Words	2
12	C; C	U1L2: Comprehension: Author's Purpose	3
13	B	U1L2: Comprehension: Figurative Language	2
14	A	U1L1: Vocabulary Strategy: Prefixes *dis-, ex-, inter-, non-*	2
15	C; D	U1L2: Comprehension: Author's Purpose	3
16	3, 2, 5, 1, 4	U1L3: Comprehension: Sequence of Events	2
	See rubric on p. T26.	U1L5: Comprehension: Fact and Opinion	4
17	Sample two-point response: The author claims that pollution and warmer temperatures are a threat to the Inuit people. This claim is supported with examples and facts. The author states, "The Arctic cold traps these chemicals in the air and water for decades. The pollution then shows up in local wildlife." This supports the claim that pollution is a threat to the Inuit. The author also states, "In addition, this melting ice may have a harmful effect on drinking water sources." This supports the claim that warmer temperatures are a threat to the Inuit people.		
	Sample one-point response: The author claims that pollution and warmer temperatures are a threat to the Inuit people.		
18	C	U1L2: Vocabulary Strategy: Suffixes *-er, -or, -ar, -ist, -ian, -ent*	2
19	B; D	U1L2: Comprehension: Author's Purpose	3
20	A, B, C	U1L5: Comprehension: Fact and Opinion	3
	See rubric on p. T26.	U1L5: Comprehension: Analyze Events	3
21	Sample two-point response: The author illustrates, through an anecdote of a burning apartment building, what happens when a fire is discovered. The anecdote begins with people noticing the fire. It continues with the arrival of the fire brigade. It includes a description of what the firefighters wear. The anecdote concludes with a description of the firefighters using hoses, fire trucks, and hydrants to extinguish the fire.		
	Sample one-point response: The author illustrates, through an anecdote of a burning apartment building, what happens when a fire is discovered.		

Item Number	Correct Answer	Unit, Lesson, Program Skill	Depth of Knowledge
		WRITING	
22	rythym, blunndar	U1L1: Spelling: Short Vowels	1
23	D	U1L3: Spelling: Vowel Sounds /oi/	1
24	D	U1L1: Grammar: Complete Sentences	2
25	See answer below.	U1L4: Writing: Organization	2
	Maria was also excited . . . , Later, Maria and her family . . .		
26	A, F	U1L2: Writing: Elaboration	2
27	D	U1L4: Grammar: Proper and Common Nouns	1
28	B	U1L2: Grammar: Kinds of Sentences	2
29	A	U1L2: Writing: Elaboration	2
30	D	U1L4: Writing: Organization	2
31	See rubric on p. T26.	U1L5: Writing: Elaboration	3
	Sample two-point response: I have always been enamored with the ocean, loving to spend as much time as possible there. My parents taught us how to swim when we were extremely young, and from that day, it was difficult to get me out of the water. One day while swimming I felt a terrible stinging sensation. Initially I ignored the feeling, but then it started to feel exceptionally painful, so I exited the water to locate my parents. I showed them where I felt the sting. The area was already inflamed.		
	Sample one-point response: I have always truly enjoyed being in the ocean. My parents gave us instruction on how to swim when we were babies, and you could always find me there as soon as I had learned. One day, I went for a swim, and I felt something sting me. At first, I just ignored it, but then it started to throb a lot. In pain, I got out of the water to find my parents, and showed them where the sting was. The area was huge in a matter of minutes.		
		LISTENING	
32	D	U1L2: Speaking and Listening: Identify Ideas and Supporting Evidence	2
33	D, E	U1L2: Speaking and Listening: Identify Ideas and Supporting Evidence	3
34	C, D	U1L2: Speaking and Listening: Identify Ideas and Supporting Evidence	1
35	B, D	U1L2: Speaking and Listening: Identify Ideas and Supporting Evidence	3
36	C	U1L2: Speaking and Listening: Identify Ideas and Supporting Evidence	1
37	D; B	U1L2: Speaking and Listening: Identify Ideas and Supporting Evidence	2
38	A; D	U1L2: Speaking and Listening: Identify Ideas and Supporting Evidence	3

Item Number	Correct Answer	Unit, Lesson, Program Skill	Depth of Knowledge
39	A	U1L2: Speaking and Listening: Identify Ideas and Supporting Evidence	2
40	C	U1L2: Speaking and Listening: Identify Ideas and Supporting Evidence	1
RESEARCH			
41	A, C	U1L3: Comprehension: Diagrams	2
42	stratus, nimbostratus, stratocumulus	U1L3: Comprehension: Diagrams	2
43	C	U1L5: Comprehension: Author's Purpose	2
44	See answer below.	U1L5: Comprehension: Author's Purpose	2
we must not discount the negative effect MP3s have had on the music industry			
45	A, D	U1L5: Comprehension: Author's Purpose	2

Performance Task 1

Item Number	Correct Answer	Unit, Lesson, Program Skill	Depth of Knowledge
1	See rubric on p. T26.	U1L5: Comprehension: Author's Purpose	4
	Sample two-point response: Both articles are written to inform the reader about Vikings, with a focus on the Vikings as explorers. Source #1 explains how Vikings explored new land, traveled the coast of Europe, and headed inland to Germany, France, and Spain. Source #2 explains how the Vikings came to North America. The authors' purposes are different, as demonstrated by the other information each author focuses on. In Source #1, the author explains how the Vikings were raiders, while Source #2 explains how a couple worked to prove that Vikings came to North America.		
	Sample one-point response: The authors' purposes for Sources #1 and #2 are similar because both are written to inform the reader about Vikings. Source #1 explains how Vikings explored new land, traveled the coast of Europe, and headed inland to Germany, France, and Spain. Source #2 explains how the Vikings came to North America.		
2	See rubric on p. T26.	U2L10: Comprehension: Arguments and Claims	4
	Sample two-point response: Source #1 explains how Vikings lived by focusing on their roles as explorers and raiders. The claim that Vikings were explorers is backed up with the fact that Vikings were the first Europeans to reach North America and build a settlement. The claim of Vikings as raiders is backed up with examples of how Vikings would find new land to settle, take what they wanted, and kill the people who were already there. Through the description of the discovery of a skeleton, Source #3 explains how Vikings once lived. One claim in this passage is that a common fighting technique of the Vikings was a blow to the leg. The knife wound found in the skeleton's thigh supports this claim.		
	Sample one-point response: Source #1 explains that Vikings were explorers and raiders. Viking explorers were the first Europeans to reach North America and build a settlement. Viking raiders would find new land to settle, take what they wanted, and kill the people who were already there.		
3	See answer below.	U2L10: Comprehension: Arguments and Claims	3
	Row 1: X in all three columns; Row 2: X in column 2 only; Row 3: X in column 3 only		
Essay Response	See rubric on p. T27.	U2L10: Writing: Narrative	4

Assessment 2

Item Number	Correct Answer	Unit, Lesson, Program Skill	Depth of Knowledge
		READING	
1	A, C	U2L9: Vocabulary Strategy: Denotation and Connotation	3
2	A	U2L7: Comprehension: Text and Graphic Features	2
3	C	U3L11: Comprehension: Sequence of Events	2
4	C	U3L13: Comprehension: Main Ideas and Details	3
5	C	U3L11: Vocabulary Strategy: Suffixes *-ion, -ation, -ism*	1
6	B	U2L10: Comprehension: Author's Purpose	3
7	B	U2L7: Comprehension: Figurative Language	3
8	A	U3L11: Comprehension: Arguments and Claims	3
9	B	U3L13: Comprehension: Domain-Specific Vocabulary	2
10	A, B, E	U3L11: Comprehension: Sequence of Events	3
11	C; A	U3L13: Comprehension: Main Ideas and Details	2
12	A	U2L6: Vocabulary Strategy: Using Context	2
13	D	U3L11: Vocabulary Strategy: Suffixes *-ion, -ation, -ism*	2
14	A; D	U2L6: Comprehension: Theme	3
15	While you have been chatting	U2L9: Comprehension: Style and Tone	3
16	See rubric on p. T26.	U2L9: Comprehension: Cause and Effect	3
16	Sample two-point response: Diego, Marvin, and Ailaisha repeat their experiment for two reasons. First, they do not get the results they expected. According to their research, when they plot the data, they should see a line that ascends right to indicate a positive correlation between stress levels and temperature. The graph of their results shows a negative correlation. Second, Marvin discovers that the participants were sitting under an air-conditioning vent, which kept them cool and skewed the data.		
	Sample one-point response: Diego, Marvin, and Ailaisha repeat their experiment for two reasons. First, they do not get the results they expected. Second, Marvin discovers that the participants were sitting under an air-conditioning vent.		
17	B	U3L13: Vocabulary Strategy: Figures of Speech	2
18	See answer below.	U2L6: Comprehension: Understanding Characters	3
	Bo, I am so sorry...; Without you, I don't know ...		
19	C	U2L8: Comprehension: Conclusions and Generalizations	2
20	See rubric on p. T26.	U2L6: Comprehension: Theme	4
20	Sample two-point response: The theme is never judge someone or something by appearances. Grandma Sarey says that Bo looks "like a big wolf" and takes up a lot space. She also lifts her skirt out of the way so he won't step on it. She doesn't like him. However, when Bo rescues her, she realizes that Bo is a valuable part of the family even though he is big and scary looking.		
	Sample one-point response: The theme is never judge someone or something by appearances.		
21	C, D, E	U2L6: Comprehension: Understanding Characters	2

Item Number	Correct Answer	Unit, Lesson, Program Skill	Depth of Knowledge
WRITING			
22	shuderred, forgeting	U2L9: Spelling: Words with *-ed* or *-ing*	1
23	D	U3L14: Spelling: Word Parts: *com-*, *con-*	1
24	B	U2L8: Grammar: Coordinating Conjunctions	2
25	See answer below.	U2L7: Writing: Organization	1
	One of the hardest things to do is to bathe a new baby. Companies should not complain about maternity leave, because that should be a given.		
26	A, C, F	U2L6: Writing: Elaboration	2
27	A	U3L11: Grammar: Subject and Object Pronouns	2
28	C	U2L7: Grammar: Verbs and Objects	2
29	C	U3L15: Writing: Elaboration	2
30	C	U3L12: Writing: Elaboration	2
31	See rubric on p. T26.	U3L13: Writing: Organization	3
	Sample two-point response: French toast is not only delicious, it is also extremely easy to prepare. There are few ingredients, and the steps are quite simple.		
	Sample one-point response: There are several steps required to make French toast.		
LISTENING			
32	C	U2L7: Speaking and Listening: Identify and Interpret Purpose, Central Idea, and Key Points	3
33	A, E	U3L13: Speaking and Listening: Identify Ideas and Supporting Evidence	1
34	See answer below.	U2L7: Speaking and Listening: Identify and Interpret Purpose, Central Idea, and Key Points	1
	Men = practice archery and repair animal pens; Women = bring silk to market; Children = watch over animals		
35	D	U2L7: Speaking and Listening: Identify and Interpret Purpose, Central Idea, and Key Points	3
36	B	U2L7: Speaking and Listening: Identify and Interpret Purpose, Central Idea, and Key Points	1
37	C; A	U2L7: Speaking and Listening: Identify and Interpret Purpose, Central Idea, and Key Points	2
38	C	U2L7: Speaking and Listening: Identify and Interpret Purpose, Central Idea, and Key Points	1
39	D	U3L13: Speaking and Listening: Identify Ideas and Supporting Evidence	2
40	A, B, E	U2L7: Speaking and Listening: Identify and Interpret Purpose, Central Idea, and Key Points	3

Item Number	Correct Answer	Unit, Lesson, Program Skill	Depth of Knowledge
		RESEARCH	
41	A, F	U2L7: Comprehension: Text and Graphic Features	2
42	See answer below.	U2L10: Comprehension: Arguments and Claims	2
	Brushaway toothpaste contains a special ingredient that helps rid your teeth of unwanted plaque. With everyday use, Brushaway toothpaste will also keep your teeth their natural bright white color. Moreover, Brushaway's special combination of ingredients makes your breath fresh.		
43	C	U2L10: Comprehension: Author's Purpose	2
44	A, B, C	U3L15: Comprehension: Text and Graphic Features	2
45	1. to entertain 2. to inform 3. to persuade	U2L10: Comprehension: Author's Purpose	2

Performance Task 2

Item Number	Correct Answer	Unit, Lesson, Program Skill	Depth of Knowledge
1	See rubric on p. T26.	U4L19: Comprehension: Cause and Effect	4
	Sample two-point response: Many events contributed to the rise of the civil rights movement. Source #2 explains how the actions of Rosa Parks led to the desegregation of the bus system. Source #3 explains how *Brown v. Board of Education* affected the integration of schools. Both of these events were victories for civil rights.		
	Sample one-point response: The march from Selma brought attention to the difficulties African Americans encountered while trying to vote.		
2	See rubric on p. T26.	U4L19: Comprehension: Conclusions and Generalizations	4
	Sample two-point response: Responses to the civil rights movement were mixed. Many people supported the movement, but others did not. Rosa Parks' refusal to give up her seat resulted in a bus boycott. After the case of *Brown v. Board of Education*, the Arkansas governor still did not want blacks to be admitted to the school. Black students eventually had to be escorted by federal troops into a predominantly white school.		
	Sample one-point response: The Supreme Court found that separate educational facilities were unequal. This shows the Supreme Court supported the civil rights movement.		
3	See answer below.	U4L16: Comprehension: Author's Purpose	3
	Row 1: Sources #1, #2, #3; Row 2: Source #2; Row 3: Source #3; Row 4: Source #1		
Essay Response	See rubric on p. T28.	U3L15: Writing: Informative	4

Assessment 3

Item Number	Correct Answer	Unit, Lesson, Program Skill	Depth of Knowledge
		READING	
1	A	U5L23: Vocabulary Strategy: Using Context	2
2	A, B, C	U5L25: Comprehension: Sequence of Events	3
3	C, D	U4L20: Comprehension: Analyze Events	3
4	See answer below.	U4L19: Comprehension: Conclusions and Generalizations	3
	The contrast between Hannah's ...; She had a warm, safe home…; Hannah worked with her mother ...		
5	B	U5L22: Vocabulary Strategy: Denotation and Connotation	2
6	A	U5L24: Comprehension: Author's Purpose	2
7	A	U4L17: Comprehension: Figurative Language	1
8	B, C	U4L19: Comprehension: Analyze Historical Characters	3
9	A	U4L20: Vocabulary Strategy: Prefixes *un-, re-, in-, im-, ir-, il-*	2
10	D; B	U4L20: Comprehension: Main Ideas and Details	3
11	See rubric on p. T26.	U4L17: Comprehension: Fact and Opinion	4
	Sample two-point response: Yes, the claim that President Kennedy's decision to focus on landing on the moon was a shrewd move is supported by reasons and evidence. The text says that "Accomplishing this [landing on the moon] would require both countries to develop different rockets and new technology, giving the Americans an even chance to compete." The text also says that "In addition, landing on the moon would be an amazing, morale-boosting achievement for the United States." Both of these details support the claim.		
	Sample one-point response: Yes, the claim that President Kennedy's decision to focus on landing on the moon was a shrewd move is supported by reasons and evidence.		
12	A	U5L25: Comprehension: Sequence of Events	3
13	B	U5L25: Vocabulary Strategy: Suffixes *-able, -ible*	2
14	The airport is still closed ...	U4L18: Comprehension: Analyze Setting	3
15	A; B	U5L21: Comprehension: Compare and Contrast	3
16	C	U4L18: Comprehension: Author's Word Choice	2
17	D	U5L24: Vocabulary Strategy: Prefixes *con-, com-, pre-, pro-*	2
18	A; D	U5L21: Comprehension: Point of View	3
19	B	U5L21: Vocabulary Strategy: Word Relationships	2

Item Number	Correct Answer	Unit, Lesson, Program Skill	Depth of Knowledge
20	See rubric on p. T26.	U5L23: Comprehension: Understanding Characters	3
	Sample two-point response: Yes, the school orchestra becomes important to Felicia. One reason is that Felicia dreams of belonging to an orchestra. The text says, "It would be like an actual dream come true" and "really want to be a famous cellist." Another reason is that she thinks the orchestra might help her find her place in school. The text says, "but I also want to be in the orchestra because then maybe I would feel a part of this school."		
	Sample one-point response: Yes, the school orchestra becomes important to Felicia.		
21	A	U5L23: Comprehension: Figurative Language	2
WRITING			
22	visable, enjoyible	U4L17: Spelling: Suffixes: -able/-ible, -ate	1
23	C	U5L22: Spelling: Words with Silent Letters	1
24	D	U4L19: Grammar: Punctuation	2
25	See answer below.	U4L19: Writing: Organization	1
	My parents took ...; My family loved ...		
26	A, C, D	U5L21: Writing: Elaboration	2
27	B	U5L22: Grammar: Punctuation and Quotations	2
28	D	U4L17: Grammar: More Kinds of Pronouns	2
29	A	U4L16: Writing: Elaboration	2
30	D	U5L25: Writing: Elaboration	2
31	See rubric on p. T26.	U4L19: Writing: Organization	3
	Sample two-point response: Being responsible for a child's health and well-being is a serious matter.		
	Sample one-point response: Finally, babysitters should also be aware of any health conditions the children have, such as allergies.		
LISTENING			
32	B	U4L19: Speaking and Listening: Identify and Interpret Purpose, Central Idea, and Key Points	1
33	A, C, D	U4L19: Speaking and Listening: Identify and Interpret Purpose, Central Idea, and Key Points	2

Item Number	Correct Answer	Unit, Lesson, Program Skill	Depth of Knowledge
34	C	U5L23: Speaking and Listening: Draw and Support Conclusions	3
35	A	U4L19: Speaking and Listening: Identify and Interpret Purpose, Central Idea, and Key Points	1
36	A; D	U5L23: Speaking and Listening: Draw and Support Conclusions	3
37	B	U4L19: Speaking and Listening: Identify and Interpret Purpose, Central Idea, and Key Points	2
38	C	U4L19: Speaking and Listening: Identify and Interpret Purpose, Central Idea, and Key Points	1
39	A, B	U5L23: Speaking and Listening: Draw and Support Conclusions	3
40	See answer below.	U4L19: Speaking and Listening: Identify and Interpret Purpose, Central Idea, and Key Points	2
	Qin Dynasty, Qin Dynasty, Han Dynasty, Han Dynasty		
RESEARCH			
41	B, D, F	U5L22: Comprehension: Conclusions and Generalizations	2
42	See answer below.	U4L19: Comprehension: Cause and Effect	2
	uproot trees ...; destroy buildings ...; wash away entire beaches		
43	A	U4L16: Comprehension: Author's Purpose	2
44	A, B, D	U4L19: Comprehension: Conclusions and Generalizations	2
45	See answer below.	U5L24: Comprehension: Author's Purpose	2
	Even though it would come at a cost ...		

Performance Task 3

Item Number	Correct Answer	Unit, Lesson, Program Skill	Depth of Knowledge
1	See rubric on p. T26.	U5L22: Comprehension: Conclusions and Generalizations	4
	Sample two-point response: Robots have changed the lives of people in many ways. Source #1 explains that some people use robots as friends and some people use robots to help them lose weight. Source #2 explains that some robots may be used for space research, while others descend into volcanoes.		
	Sample one-point response: Some are used to go places that people cannot go, such as space and inside volcanoes.		
2	See rubric on p. T26.	U5L24: Comprehension: Author's Purpose	4
	Sample two-point response: Source #1 was written to persuade readers that humanlike robots offer many benefits to society. Source #2 was written to inform readers about the history of robots. Source #3 was written to persuade readers that despite the many benefits of robots, there are many potential problems with robots that society should consider as advances in technology are made. Sources #1 and #3 are similar in that they are both written to persuade the reader. However, they differ on what they are trying to persuade the reader to believe. Source #1 focuses on the positive aspects of robots, while Source #3 focuses on the negative. Sources #1 and #2 are alike in that both reference the positive effects of robots. They are different in that Source #1 was written to persuade, while Source #2 was written to inform.		
	Sample one-point response: Source #1 was written to persuade. Source #2 was written to inform. Source #3 was written to persuade. Sources #1 and #3 are alike because they are both written to persuade. They are different in that Source #1 is about the benefits of robots, while Source #3 is about the dangers of robots.		
3	C, D, E	U5L22: Comprehension: Conclusions and Generalizations	3
Essay Response	See rubric on p. T29.	U5L25: Writing: Argumentative	4

Constructed-Response Rubrics

READING Rubric

Score of 2	• The response is logical and has an identifiable pattern/sequence. • The response provides adequate evidence of the student's ability to interpret information and/or make inferences and conclusions about the passage. • The response references clear evidence from the text that supports the student's response. • The response includes specific examples and/or details that relate to the text.
Score of 1	• The response is logical and connected to the prompt but may lack an identifiable pattern/sequence. • The response provides limited evidence of the student's ability to interpret information and/or make inferences and conclusions. • The response references little evidence from the text that supports the student's response. • The response includes some examples and/or details that relate to the text.
Score of 0	• The response provides no evidence of the student's ability to interpret information and/or make inferences and conclusions. • The response includes no relevant information, evidence, or examples from the text.

WRITING Rubric

Score of 2	• The response is logical, has an identifiable pattern/sequence, and is connected to the prompt. • The response provides and incorporates sufficient key points, reasons, details, and/or evidence to support the student's response. • The response includes elaboration and uses precise and specific words, language, and details.
Score of 1	• The response is mostly logical and connected to the prompt but may lack an identifiable pattern/sequence. • The response provides and incorporates limited key points, reasons, details, and/or evidence to support the student's response. • The response includes limited elaboration and uses general words, language, and details.
Score of 0	• The response has a weak or no connection to the prompt, may contradict the details/information in the prompt, or may restate provided details, introduce new or irrelevant details/information, or summarize the prompt. • The response gives no or an inappropriate opinion/introduction/central idea/conclusion and provides few or no key points, reasons, details, and/or evidence. • The response includes no elaboration and uses poor word choice.

Performance Task: Narrative Writing Rubric

Purpose/Organization

Score	4	3	2	1	NS
Purpose/Organization	**The narrative is clear, focused, and well organized throughout.** • Contains an effective and complete plot • Develops a strong setting, narrator/characters • Includes a variety of transitions to connect ideas • Contains a logical sequence of events • Includes an effective introduction and conclusion	**The narrative's organization is adequately maintained, and the focus is generally clear.** • Plot is mostly effective/may contain small flaws • Develops setting/narrator/characters • Adequate use of transitions to connect ideas • Contains an adequate sequence of events • Includes adequate introduction and conclusion	**The narrative is somewhat organized and may be unclear in some parts. Plot may be inconsistent.** • Minimal development of setting, narrator/characters • Inconsistent use of transitions to connect ideas • Sequence of events is weak or unclear • Introduction and conclusion need improvement	**The narrative's focus and organization are not clear.** • Little or no plot • Little or no development of setting, narrator/characters • Contains few or inappropriate transitions and weak connections among ideas • Sequence of events is not organized • Introduction and/or conclusion may be missing	• Not intelligible • Not written in English • Not on topic • Contains text copied from source • Does not address the purpose for writing

Development/Elaboration

Score	4	3	2	1	NS
Development/Elaboration	**The narrative includes effective elaboration using details, dialogue, and description.** • Characters, setting, experiences, and events are well developed • Links to sources may enrich the narrative • Writer uses a variety of narrative techniques that strengthen the story or illustrate the experience • Contains effective sensory, concrete, and figurative language • Style is appropriate and effective	**The narrative includes adequate elaboration using details, dialogue, and description.** • Characters, setting, experiences, and events are adequately developed • Links to sources may contribute to the narrative • Writer uses a variety of narrative techniques that generally move the story forward and illustrate the experience • Contains adequate sensory, concrete, and figurative language • Style is mostly appropriate	**The narrative includes partial or ineffective elaboration using unclear or inconsistent details, dialogue, and description.** • Characters, setting, experiences, and events lack consistent development • Links to sources may be unsuccessful but do not detract from the narrative • Writer uses inconsistent or weak narrative techniques • Contains weak sensory, concrete, and figurative language • Style is inconsistent or inappropriate	**The narrative provides little or no elaboration using few or no details, dialogue, and description.** • Very little development of characters, setting, experiences, and events • Links to sources, if present, may interfere with the narrative • Writer's use of narrative techniques are minimal and may be incorrect • Little or no sensory, concrete, and figurative language • Little or no evidence of style	• Not intelligible • Not written in English • Not on topic • Contains text copied from source • Does not address the purpose for writing

Conventions

Score	2	1	0	NS
Conventions	**The narrative demonstrates adequate command of conventions.** • Consistent use of correct sentence structures, punctuation, capitalization, grammar, and spelling	**The narrative demonstrates partial command of conventions.** • Limited use of correct sentence structures, punctuation, capitalization, grammar, and spelling	**The narrative demonstrates little or no command of conventions.** • Rare use of correct sentence structures, punctuation, capitalization, grammar, and spelling	• Not intelligible • Not written in English • Not on topic • Contains text copied from source

Performance Task: Informative/Explanatory Writing Rubric

Score	4	3	2	1	NS
Purpose/Organization	**The response is clear, focused, and well organized throughout.** • Main or central idea is clear, focused, and effective for task, audience, and purpose • Includes a variety of transitions to relate ideas • Contains a logical sequence of ideas with strong relationships between them • Includes an effective introduction and conclusion	**The response's organization is adequately maintained, and the focus is generally clear.** • Main or central idea is clear, mostly focused, and mostly effective for task, audience, and purpose • Includes some variety of transitions to relate ideas • Contains an adequate sequence of ideas with adequate relationships between them • Includes an adequate introduction and conclusion	**The response is somewhat focused but may be unclear in parts. Organization may be inconsistent.** • Main or central idea may be somewhat unclear, may lack focus, or may be ineffective for task, audience, and purpose • Includes little variety of transitions to relate ideas • Sequence of ideas may be weak or unclear • Introduction and conclusion need improvement	**The response's focus and organization are not clear.** • Main or central idea may be confusing; response may be inappropriate for task, audience, and purpose • Includes few or no transitions to relate ideas • Sequence of ideas is unorganized; may include off-topic ideas • Introduction and/or conclusion may be missing	• Not intelligible • Not written in English • Not on topic • Contains text copied from source • Does not address the purpose for writing
Evidence/Elaboration	**The response presents strong support for the main and supporting ideas with effective use of evidence from sources, facts, and details, elaborating with specific and effective language.** • Evidence from sources is integrated, is relevant, and supports key ideas • Writer uses a variety of elaborative techniques • Vocabulary is clear and appropriate for task, audience, and purpose • Style is appropriate and effective	**The response presents adequate support for the main and supporting ideas with evidence from sources, facts, and details, adequately elaborating with a mix of specific and general language.** • Evidence from sources is integrated, is relevant, and adequately supports key ideas • Writer uses some elaborative techniques • Vocabulary is mostly appropriate for task, audience, and purpose • Style is generally appropriate and effective	**The response presents inconsistent support for the main and supporting ideas with limited evidence from sources, facts, and details. Elaboration is inconsistent with simple language.** • Evidence from sources may be poorly integrated or irrelevant, or only loosely supports key ideas • Writer uses few elaborative techniques • Vocabulary is somewhat inappropriate for task, audience, and purpose • Style is largely ineffective	**The response presents little support for the main and supporting ideas with little or no evidence from sources, facts, or details. Elaboration is inadequate or absent.** • Evidence from sources, if present, may be irrelevant with little support for key ideas • Writer uses few or no elaborative techniques • Vocabulary is inappropriate for task, audience, and purpose • Style is weak or absent	• Not intelligible • Not written in English • Not on topic • Contains text copied from source • Does not address the purpose for writing

Score	2	1	0	NS
Conventions	**The response demonstrates adequate command of conventions.** • Consistent use of correct sentence structures, punctuation, capitalization, grammar, and spelling	**The response demonstrates partial command of conventions.** • Limited use of correct sentence structures, punctuation, capitalization, grammar, and spelling	**The response demonstrates little or no command of conventions.** • Rare use of correct sentence structures, punctuation, capitalization, grammar, and spelling	• Not intelligible • Not written in English • Not on topic • Contains text copied from source

Performance Task: Argument Writing Rubric

Score	4	3	2	1	NS
Purpose/Organization	**The response is clear, focused, and well organized throughout.** • Argument is clear, focused, effective for task, audience, and purpose • Includes a variety of transitions to relate ideas • Contains a logical sequence of ideas with strong relationships between them • Includes an effective introduction and conclusion	**The response's organization is adequately maintained, and the focus is generally clear.** • Argument is clear, mostly focused, and mostly effective for task, audience, and purpose • Includes some variety of transitions to relate ideas • Contains an adequate sequence of ideas with adequate relationships between them • Includes an adequate introduction and conclusion	**The response is somewhat focused but may be unclear in parts. Organization may be inconsistent.** • Argument may be somewhat unclear, lack focus, or be ineffective for task, audience, and purpose • Includes little variety of transitions to relate ideas • Sequence of ideas may be weak or unclear • Introduction and conclusion need improvement	**The response's focus and organization are not clear.** • Argument may be confusing; response may be inappropriate for task, audience, and purpose • Includes few or no transitions to relate ideas • Sequence of ideas is unorganized; may include off-topic ideas • Introduction and/or conclusion may be missing	• Not intelligible • Not written in English • Not on topic • Contains text copied from source • Does not address the purpose for writing
Evidence/Elaboration	**The response presents strong support for the argument with effective use of evidence from sources, facts, and details, elaborating with specific and effective language.** • Evidence from sources is integrated, is relevant, and supports key ideas • Writer uses a variety of elaborative techniques • Vocabulary is clear and appropriate for task, audience, and purpose • Style is appropriate and effective	**The response presents adequate support for the opinion with evidence from sources, facts, and details, adequately elaborating with a mix of specific and general language.** • Evidence from sources is integrated, is relevant, and adequately supports key ideas • Writer uses some elaborative techniques • Vocabulary is mostly appropriate for task, audience, and purpose • Style is generally appropriate and effective	**The response presents inconsistent support for the argument with limited evidence from sources, facts, and details. Elaboration is inconsistent with simple language.** • Evidence from sources may be poorly integrated or irrelevant or only loosely supports key ideas • Writer uses few elaborative techniques • Vocabulary is somewhat inappropriate for task, audience, and purpose • Style is largely ineffective	**The response presents little support for the argument with little or no evidence from sources, facts, or details. Elaboration is inadequate or absent.** • Evidence from sources, if present, may be irrelevant, with little support for key ideas • Writer uses few or no elaborative techniques • Vocabulary is inappropriate for task, audience, and purpose • Style is weak or absent	• Not intelligible • Not written in English • Not on topic • Contains text copied from source • Does not address the purpose for writing

Score	2	1	0	NS
Conventions	**The response demonstrates adequate command of conventions.** • Consistent use of correct sentence structures, punctuation, capitalization, grammar, and spelling	**The response demonstrates partial command of conventions.** • Limited use of correct sentence structures, punctuation, capitalization, grammar, and spelling	**The response demonstrates little or no command of conventions.** • Rare use of correct sentence structures, punctuation, capitalization, grammar, and spelling	• Not intelligible • Not written in English • Not on topic • Contains text copied from source

Test Record Form

Student Name _____

Assessment 1   Date _____

Date Administered _____		Possible Score	Acceptable Score	Student Score
Reading (Items 1–21)*	Selected-Response	19	17	
	Constructed-Response	4		
Writing (Items 22–31)*	Selected-Response	9	8	
	Constructed-Response	2		
Listening (Items 32–40)		9	7	
Research (Items 41–45)		5	4	
Total		48	36	
FINAL SCORE = Total Student Score x 2.08 = _____				

Performance Task 1   Date _____

Date Administered _____		Possible Score	Acceptable Score	Student Score
Part 1 (Items 1–3)*	Selected-Response	1	4	
	Constructed-Response	4		
Part 2 (Essay Response)		10	7	
Total		15	11	
Total Student Score x 6.67 = _____				

Assessment 2   Date _____

Date Administered _____		Possible Score	Acceptable Score	Student Score
Reading (Items 1–21)*	Selected-Response	19	17	
	Constructed-Response	4		
Writing (Items 22–31)*	Selected-Response	9	8	
	Constructed-Response	2		
Listening (Items 32–40)		9	7	
Research (Items 41–45)		5	4	
Total		48	36	
FINAL SCORE = Total Student Score x 2.08 = _____				

Performance Task 2   Date _____

Date Administered _____		Possible Score	Acceptable Score	Student Score
Part 1 (Items 1–3)*	Selected-Response	1	4	
	Constructed-Response	4		
Part 2 (Essay Response)		10	7	
Total		15	11	
Total Student Score x 6.67 = _____				

Assessment 3   Date _____

Date Administered _____		Possible Score	Acceptable Score	Student Score
Reading (Items 1–21)*	Selected-Response	19	17	
	Constructed-Response	4		
Writing (Items 22–31)*	Selected-Response	9	8	
	Constructed-Response	2		
Listening (Items 32–40)		9	7	
Research (Items 41–45)		5	4	
Total		48	36	
FINAL SCORE = Total Student Score x 2.08 = _____				

Performance Task 3   Date _____

Date Administered _____		Possible Score	Acceptable Score	Student Score
Part 1 (Items 1–3)*	Selected-Response	1	4	
	Constructed-Response	4		
Part 2 (Essay Response)		10	7	
Total		15	11	
Total Student Score x 6.67 = _____				

*This section includes constructed-response items worth up to two points each. Please note when scoring.

Name _____ Date _____

Assessment 1
Reading

Read the text. Then answer the questions.

How to Write a Play

Izzie paced furiously up and down the length of her bedroom, sighing and shaking her head. "Izzie," her mother called from downstairs, "stop, or you will wear a hole in the carpet."

"But Mom, you don't understand. I have to write a play for a prominent literary competition, and I have the worst case of writer's block in history! My brain is like a black hole in the universe where ideas are sucked in, never to be seen again. I have no idea where to begin!"

Izzie heard her mother ascend the stairs. "Listen, honey," said her mother calmly. "A very wise teacher once told me to write about what I know. Have a snack to give you energy, close your eyes, reflect on events in your own life, and inspiration will come to you."

After her mother left, Izzie drew a deep breath. She arranged the pillows on her bed and reclined comfortably, letting thoughts drift randomly through her mind. Suddenly, she bolted upright. "Eureka!" she exclaimed. "I know exactly what to write about!" Izzie ran to her computer, threw herself into her chair, and frantically began to tap the keys. An hour later, she flexed her fingers, scrolled to the first page, and reread her script. "Hmm, I have a realistic main character and likeable minor characters. I have a strong plot that unfolds in a series of episodes, and I have a specific conflict that is logically resolved. In addition, I have included lively dialogue, informative stage directions, and a variety of settings. Not bad for a first draft," she said proudly. "Hey, Mom!" she called. "Would you like to hear an excerpt from my fantastic, fabulous, and funny play?" Hearing her mother's affirmative reply, Izzie unplugged her laptop and took it with her to the kitchen.

"Okay," she announced, "the setting of the first scene is the main character's bedroom, and as the play opens, the main character, a sixth grader named Petra, is slumped at her desk with a look of despair on her face. Here goes."

Petra: *(sighing deeply)* What am I going to do? My deadline for this play is approaching in two days. So far, I have written a knockoff of a famous book that features a scarecrow losing his stuffing, kicking a tin can, and chasing a Siamese cat. Then, I sketched out a plot that involves Tinkerbell flitting around a jar of peanut butter, thinking it was Peter Pan, and then I came to my senses and realized that it could only lead to a sticky end. Finally, I came up with the idea to have a poor girl meet a prince and turn into a princess, but desperate as I am, even I have to admit that story line might be a little tired. Woe is me!

Mom: *(entering the bedroom from stage right)* Petra, I hate to see you frustrated. You have been working so hard to write this play that I think that you need to take a break and let your creativity recharge.

Petra: The clock is ticking on this opportunity. I have always wanted to be a writer, and this is my big chance. Every other day, I come up with myriad ideas— so many, I can't even count them! So why does trying to write this play make me feel like I am trying to climb out of quicksand?

Mom: *(patting Petra's shoulder)* For what it is worth, here is my advice, which was first given to me by one of my favorite teachers: Write about what you know, and keep it real. Now eat this apple. It will give you energy and help you get yourself back on track. *(Mom smiles and exits.)*

Petra: *(looking thoughtful)* Mom has a point. Maybe I have been trying to make my play too far-fetched. Let me think. *(pausing)* Eureka! I have an idea.

Izzie looked up grinning as her mother clapped vigorously. "Of course, that is only the first scene, Mom. Petra writes a play that ends up getting performed for parents' night! And, just maybe," said Izzie excitedly, "mine will, too!"

---

1 First, read the dictionary definition. Then, complete the task.

> (*v*) **1.** to go up

Underline the word that **most closely** matches the definition provided.

> "But, Mom, you don't understand. I have to write a play for a prominent literary competition, and I have the worst case of writer's block in history! My brain is like a black hole in the universe where ideas are sucked in, never to be seen again. I have no idea where to begin!"

> Izzie heard her mother ascend the stairs. "Listen, honey." said her mother calmly, "A very wise teacher once told me to write about what I know. Have a snack to give you energy, close your eyes, reflect on events in your own life, and inspiration will come to you."

2 Which of the following details from the text illustrate Izzie's response to her mother's advice? Select **three** options.

Ⓐ "Izzie paced furiously up and down the length of her bedroom, sighing and shaking her head."

Ⓑ "Have a snack to give you energy, close your eyes, reflect on events in your own life, and inspiration will come to you."

Ⓒ "After her mother left, Izzie drew a deep breath."

Ⓓ "She arranged the pillows on her bed and reclined comfortably, letting thoughts drift randomly through her mind."

Ⓔ "Izzie ran to her computer, threw herself into her chair, and frantically began to tap the keys."

3 Read the sentence from the text.

My brain is like a black hole in the universe where ideas are sucked in, never to be seen again.

Which statement **best** describes what the simile in the sentence above adds to the meaning of the text?

Ⓐ It explains why Izzie is unable to write the play.

Ⓑ It illustrates Izzie's feeling of frustration with her lack of ideas.

Ⓒ It suggests that Izzie is worried that she won't win the writing competition.

Ⓓ It establishes the idea that Izzie easily gives up when she faces difficulties.

4 Read the sentence from the text.

"Hey, Mom!" she called. "Would you like to hear an excerpt from my fantastic, fabulous, and funny play?"

What tone does the author create with the use of alliteration?

Ⓐ confident

Ⓑ doubtful

Ⓒ nervous

Ⓓ somber

Name _____ Date _____

Read the text. Then answer the questions.

Quiet Heroes

"I don't know if I truly realized the jeopardy I was putting myself in by working against the Nazis," I said thoughtfully, surveying the group of students before me. They looked back at me with rapt attention. "I just knew that it was time to take a stand. My friends and I could no longer bear witness to the atrocities committed against the Jewish people without trying to help. I remember quite well the day the White Rose Society was born."

"In the crowded hallway after the dismissal of our anatomy class, Hans brushed by me, making sure to catch my eye. I nodded back surreptitiously, indicating that I remembered our meeting tonight in the basement of our medical building. If anyone found us, we were to say we were simply gathering to share <u>reflections</u> on German literature, music, and philosophy—especially those favorites of Hitler's. It was the perfect cover. The culture club that Hans had established months ago was well-known in university circles. We often invited professors, artists, musicians, and writers to speak to us. Tonight, however, there would be no guests. We would be discussing something much more potentially lethal than German cultural traditions.

With butterflies in my stomach, I made my way cautiously through the dark streets from my boarding house to the university at the appointed time. In Munich in 1942, the blackout was strictly enforced, since even the slightest ray of light could attract the Allied bombers. This meant that navigating the bumpy pavement without tripping was next to impossible, but I consoled myself with the idea that it also meant I attracted little attention, and was likely saving my life.

I reached my destination, gave the special knock on the door, and then entered quietly. My friends were already milling around, talking in hushed tones. Hans Scholl cleared his throat audibly, and called us to order, saying, 'Let's make the most of our time together. As you know, here in Munich, the situation has grown intolerable for our Jewish citizens. They have not been allowed to own businesses or property for years. Now they are being rounded up and deported to concentration camps. We have heard through very reliable sources that they live and die in horrible conditions. What can we do?'

Sophie, Hans's sister, raised her hand. 'I have an idea. I think we should start a campaign of nonviolent resistance to Nazi policies.'

I agreed immediately, thinking that Sophie's idea was perfect and wanting to give her support. 'We can print leaflets that relay the facts about what the Nazis are doing to the Jews,' I said. 'We can send them anonymously and leave them in public places without anyone seeing us. These pamphlets should explain our beliefs and rally support against the Nazis.'

I looked around, and everyone was nodding enthusiastically. Karl then reminded us that his father owned a printing press, and he could make the copies we needed for a wide distribution.

'Now, the only question is—how should we sign it?' I asked.

'I know,' said Alexander. 'We will call ourselves the White Rose Society. Our leaflets will be the *Leaves of the White Rose*. Get it?' Laughing at his cleverness, we busied ourselves planning the first edition."

I paused for a moment, reflecting on my journey into the past. We had distributed hundreds of those first leaflets, requesting that people who received them tell their friends and pass the leaflets on.

Sighing, I returned to the present. "The White Rose Society was active until 1943, but sadly, Hans and Sophie were discovered distributing pamphlets. They were arrested, and others were rounded up and interrogated, and even jailed."

The students in front of me gasped. In 1984, it was hard to imagine the kind of political repression that had held Germany in its grip more than forty years earlier.

"Was it worth it?" asked a boy in the front.

"Oh, yes," I said, reflecting for a moment on my own past in prison. "Even in my darkest moments in prison, I never regretted my actions. I just kept thinking of the words we printed on the bottom of our first leaflet: *Do not forget that every nation deserves the government it endures.*"

Name _____ Date _____

5 Read the sentence from the text.

> "If anyone found us, we were to say we were simply gathering to share <u>reflections</u> on German literature, music, and philosophy—especially those favorites of Hitler's."

What does the word <u>reflections</u> **most likely** mean?

Ⓐ an image that is seen in a mirror

Ⓑ something that shows the effect of something else

Ⓒ something that causes people to disapprove of a person

Ⓓ an opinion you form after carefully thinking about something

6 Read the sentences from the text.

> "Now they are being rounded up and <u>deported</u> to concentration camps. We have heard through very reliable sources that they live and die in horrible conditions."

What does the word <u>deported</u> **most likely** mean?

Ⓐ to make a person leave a place

Ⓑ to force out of a position of government

Ⓒ to dismiss from an organization or event

Ⓓ to exclude by general agreement of a group

7 Which episodes in the story had to take place to allow the White Rose Society to begin its campaign of nonviolent resistance? Select **three** options.

Ⓐ "We often invited professors, artists, musicians, and writers to speak to us."

Ⓑ "They were arrested, and others were rounded up and interrogated, and even jailed."

Ⓒ "The culture club that Hans had established months ago was well-known in university circles."

Ⓓ "We had distributed hundreds of those first leaflets, requesting that people who received them tell their friends and pass the leaflets on."

Ⓔ "As you know, here in Munich, the situation has grown intolerable for our Jewish citizens."

Name _____ Date _____

8 Read the sentences from the text.

> "I just knew that it was time to take a stand. My friends and I could no longer bear witness to the atrocities committed against the Jewish people without trying to help. I remember quite well the day the White Rose Society was born."

What does the dialogue reveal about the character?

Ⓐ He feels afraid about helping the Jewish people.

Ⓑ He wants to take action to help the Jewish people.

Ⓒ He wants to help the Jewish people, but he decides not to.

Ⓓ He feels that there is nothing he can do to help the Jewish people.

9 How does the narrator respond to the imprisonment of his friends?

Ⓐ He does not regret his actions.

Ⓑ He is angry with his government.

Ⓒ He wishes he had not started the society.

Ⓓ He fights harder to help the Jewish people.

Read the text. Then answer the questions.

Positive and Negative Numbers

Numbers are ideas that represent the quantity, the order, or some characteristics of objects. For example, we can say *five* apples, the *third* apple on the right, or the apple weighing *five* ounces.

If we start out with five apples and someone eats all of them, there are no apples left. That seems like a simple idea, but it took hundreds of years for people to develop the symbol *0*, or zero, to stand for "nothing" in a number. Numbers representing a quantity more than zero are called *positive numbers*. Hundreds of years ago, mathematicians began to use the idea of numbers less than zero to solve certain problems. These numbers are called *negative numbers*.

An easy way to visualize positive and negative numbers is with a number line. Zero is in the middle of the line. Positive numbers are to the right of zero, and negative numbers are to the left. The line extends infinitely in both directions. Values on the line increase from left to right. That means that 6 is greater than –3, but –3 is greater than –6.

```
 ← +—+—+—+—+—+—+—+—+—+—+—+—+—+—+—+—+—+—+—+—+—+ →
   –10 –9 –8 –7 –6 –5 –4 –3 –2 –1  0  1  2  3  4  5  6  7  8  9 10
```

There are many applications of positive and negative numbers in the real world. People use positive and negative numbers to measure temperature, determine elevation, track money, and balance electrical charges.

Measuring Temperature

On the Fahrenheit scale used in the United States, thirty-two degrees is the temperature at which water freezes. It's pretty cold when the temperature falls to zero. When the temperatures fall below zero into negative numbers, it's like being in a deep freeze. On the Celsius scale used in most other countries, zero represents freezing. That means 0°C is equal to 32°F. It also means that some negative numbers on the Celsius scale are positive numbers on the Fahrenheit scale.

Determining Elevation

Sea level is defined as the position where air and sea meet. In determining elevation, sea level is like zero on the number line. Most land is at or above sea level. The depths of the ocean are below sea level. Denver is called the Mile High City because its elevation at the state capitol is 5,280 feet, or one mile, above sea level. The Dead Sea, located between Israel and Jordan, has an elevation of about –1,300 feet, meaning it is 1,300 feet below sea level.

Name _____ Date _____

Tracking Money

When there is money in your pocket or your bank account, that's a positive number. This positive balance is called a *credit*. When you spend cash or take money out of your account, it's called a *debit*. Every time you use a debit card, you subtract money from your bank account. If you forget to keep track of all your debits, your balance might go below zero. Then you owe the bank money. You can't withdraw any more until your balance gets back on the credit side.

Balancing Electrical Charges

Everything in the world depends on the relationship of positive and negative numbers. That's because physical objects are made up of atoms, which contain particles with positive or negative electrical charges. Most of the time, these charges are balanced, so objects are neutral. For example, common table salt is made up of a positive sodium atom and a negative chlorine atom.

Static electricity lets you experience an imbalance of positive and negative electrical charges. For example, if you rub a balloon against your hair or clothes, it will stick to the wall. Because you have transferred extra negative charges to the balloon, it will be attracted to the wall, which has more positive charges relative to the balloon.

These examples show that negative numbers are not nothing. In fact, they are really something.

---

10 Look back at the number line from the text. What concept about positive and negative numbers does the number line illustrate?

Ⓐ Values on the line increase from left to right.

Ⓑ There are many applications of positive and negative numbers in the real world.

Ⓒ Everything in the world depends on the relationship of positive and negative numbers.

Ⓓ Some negative numbers on the Celsius scale are positive numbers on the Fahrenheit scale.

Name _____ Date _____

11 Read the sentence from the text.

Values on the line increase from left to right.

What does the word value **most likely** mean as it is used in this sentence?

Ⓐ a mathematical quantity

Ⓑ usefulness or importance

Ⓒ how much something costs

Ⓓ the amount of money something is worth

12 This question has two parts. First, answer part A. Then, answer part B.

Part A

What is the author's purpose for writing this text?

Ⓐ to explain how to use positive and negative numbers

Ⓑ to describe the history of positive and negative numbers

Ⓒ to give information about the usefulness of positive and negative numbers

Ⓓ to show how to use a number line to find a solution to a mathematical problem

Part B

Which detail from the text **best** supports your answer in part A?

Ⓐ "Hundreds of years ago, mathematicians began to use the idea of numbers less than zero to solve certain problems."

Ⓑ "An easy way to visualize positive and negative numbers is with a number line."

Ⓒ "There are many applications of positive and negative numbers in the real world."

Ⓓ "When there is money in your pocket or your bank account, that's a positive number."

Name _____ Date _____

13 Read the sentence from the text.

When the temperatures fall below zero into negative numbers, <u>it's like being in a deep freeze</u>.

What does the simile <u>it's like being in a deep freeze</u> mean?

Ⓐ   It is icy.

Ⓑ   It is very cold.

Ⓒ   It is not moving.

Ⓓ   It is interrupting.

Name _____ Date _____

Read the text. Then answer the questions.

Challenges for the Future

The Inuit are the native people of Canada. "Inuit" means "the people" in the Inuit language. By the year 1000 CE, they had migrated east from Russia to Alaska and then into the unspoiled land of northern Canada. In this frigid wilderness, they established their nomadic lifestyle. They hunted both sea and land mammals. They moved inland in summer and back to the coast in the winter. They respected the animals they killed and lived in harmony with their environment.

With the arrival of Europeans in the 1500s, however, the Inuit way of life began to change. Over time, the European and American hunters plundered natural resources, such as whales, leaving the Inuit struggling to survive. Diseases that were introduced by the newcomers weakened the Inuit population. Colonization by these settlers endangered the Inuit's nomadic way of life.

Until the first half of the twentieth century, the Canadian government had continued to encourage the Inuit to maintain their traditional nomadic way of life. However, many Inuit had become engaged in commercial enterprises. They were staying in one place for longer periods of time in order to take part in trading. Other Inuit began to settle in places where there were job opportunities.

By the 1950s, most Inuit had resigned themselves to moving into permanent communities. They asked the Canadian government for territory of their own. The government granted about one-third of its land to the Inuit. Nunavut, one of these communities, is in the northernmost central part of Canada. It became theirs in 1999. With land they could call their own, the Inuit gained control over their future. They experienced some benefits from this new lifestyle. They also lost many aspects of their culture as they began to live among non-Inuit people.

There are now new issues in modern society that are posing a threat to the Inuit. The practices of the industrialized world beyond Nunavut's borders have led to pollution of the environment. This is a serious problem for the Inuit, who rely so heavily on nature for their survival.

It may seem surprising that in a land without big cities, factories, or great numbers of cars, pollution is a major problem. There are several reasons for this pollution. One is that harmful chemicals produced in industrial areas to the south are carried north by wind or migrating birds. The Arctic cold then traps these chemicals in the air and water. The pollution also shows up in local wildlife.

Because the Inuit rely so heavily on local animals and fish for their food, pollution greatly affects their lives. Many chemicals that cause pollution are no longer produced, but their effects are still being felt today. The Inuit have worked for years to get hazardous chemicals banned and to make sure their food supply is safe.

Changing weather patterns that cause temperatures to rise around the globe are another threat to the Arctic ecosystem. Ice melts earlier in the spring and forms later in the fall. This makes travel unpredictable and unsafe. The Inuit have also observed that some sea ice that never melted in the past is now melting during the summer. This causes problems for Arctic animals that live on the ice, such as seals and polar bears. In addition, this melting ice may have a harmful effect on drinking water sources.

Another dangerous effect of warmer temperatures is a change in the permafrost, which may be more than 1,000 feet deep. In the past, only a foot or two of the ground thawed in the Arctic summer. Increased thawing of the permafrost is causing building foundations in coastal towns to crack.

There are around 45,000 Inuit in Canada today. They have successfully overcome many obstacles throughout their history. They have had to adapt to their environment for centuries. They have also had to fight to preserve their traditions in a world in which they are a minority. Pollution and warmer temperatures are this century's new threats to their community. The Inuit are hopeful that they can once again find ways to counteract the negative effects of progress.

14 Read the sentence from the text.

> They also lost many aspects of their culture as they began to live among <u>non-Inuit</u> people.

What does the word <u>non-Inuit</u> **most likely** mean?

- Ⓐ not Inuit
- Ⓑ between Inuit
- Ⓒ among Inuit
- Ⓓ beyond Inuit

15 This question has two parts. First, answer part A. Then, answer part B.

Part A

What is the author's purpose for writing this text?

- Ⓐ to entertain with stories of the Inuit people
- Ⓑ to explain how the Inuit people preserve their culture
- Ⓒ to give information about the problems the Inuit have faced
- Ⓓ to describe the different ways the Inuit people are fighting pollution

Part B

Which detail from the text **best** supports your answer in part A?

- Ⓐ "They respected the animals they killed and lived in harmony with their environment."
- Ⓑ "They also lost many aspects of their culture as they began to live among non-Inuit people."
- Ⓒ "Because the Inuit rely so heavily on local animals and fish for their food, pollution greatly affects their lives."
- Ⓓ "They have successfully overcome many obstacles throughout their history."

16 Label each event from the text in the order in which it happened. The first event will be labeled 1, and the last event will be labeled 5.

—— The Inuit moved into permanent communities.

—— The Europeans arrived in the 1500s.

—— The Inuit fought to have hazardous chemicals banned.

—— The Inuit migrated from Russia to northern Canada.

—— Nanavut became the Inuit territory.

17 What is one of the author's claims in the text, and how is the claim supported? Include examples from the text to support your answer.

_____

_____

_____

_____

_____

Name _____ Date _____

Read the text. Then answer the questions.

Smoke and Fire

Every day in cities and towns all across the country, fires break out. Where do fires happen? They occur in all the places that people inhabit, including where they live, where they play, and where they work. The most common cause of a fire in a house or apartment usually has something to do with cooking or heating.

According to data from the U.S. Fire Administration, in 2012

- 48.7% of residential fires were caused by cooking;
- 12.1% of residential fires were caused by heating;
- 5.6% of residential fires were unintentional or careless.

Fires that occur in homes can be caused by carelessness or inattention in the kitchen. The heating systems in homes can be another cause of many damaging fires. Fireplaces, wood stoves, and chimneys can all cause residential fires.

When a fire has been discovered, it is important for a fire brigade to respond as quickly as possible. That is the best way to avoid injury to people and damage to property. Emergency telephone numbers allow people to report fires quickly, and the sirens on firefighters' trucks smooth the way for a brigade to navigate the streets efficiently and reach a fire within minutes.

Imagine that smoke is billowing in a menacing fashion from windows on the fifth floor of an apartment building, filling the air with a peculiar stench. People on the street below notice the haze, look up to see the dark smoke, and start to yell and wave their arms. Is the building on fire? Those who look carefully can see flames darting like crimson and ochre tongues around the window frames. Yes, it's a real fire that threatens both the people in the building and the building itself!

Sirens can be heard in the distance. Someone must have used a cell phone to report the fire. Here comes the fire brigade! The fire engine and fire trucks pull up in front of the building. The firefighters are ready to start extinguishing the fire. They are all wearing protective suits, helmets, face shields, and gloves. Some of them race to attach a hose to the hydrant on the street. Luckily, no cars are parked in front of the hydrant. (Sometimes people park in front of hydrants because they can't find parking in a busy urban neighborhood, but they risk paying a fine if they are caught.) The hydrant provides a steady source of water for the firefighters' hoses. One of the fire trucks actually has machines that help distribute and pump the water up to the fire. Still, extinguishing a fire on the fifth floor will be difficult.

Firefighters must have total dedication to their jobs. Why is this so important? Fighting fires is dangerous and difficult work. Many thousands of firefighters are injured every year while fighting fires or training for their jobs. Actual fires aren't the only danger they face. For example, at the scene of a fire, some firefighters are overcome by heat exhaustion, or they strain their backs while handling fire hoses. The majority of firefighter injuries reported to the National Fire Incident Reporting System (NFIRS) are associated with residential fires.

While the main job of firefighters is putting out fires, they also work to prevent them. Has a firefighter ever visited your school or classroom? Firefighters often visit schools and workplaces to teach fire safety rules. They tell people how to prevent fires. For example, many fires are caused by flammable materials. If it is coated with a certain kind of paint, a rag that is left lying in a basement can start a blaze.

Firefighters' other responsibilities include responding to emergency medical situations. For example, firefighters may be called to a lakefront to assist in rescuing and reviving a drowning victim. To perform these kinds of rescues, firefighters train on boats and with ropes, knots, and harnesses. It is very physically demanding work.

Every year, advances lead to new and better types of firefighting equipment. However, no matter how much progress is made, fighting fires is still a difficult and dangerous job. We owe firefighters our deepest appreciation for their efforts to keep us safe.

18 Read the sentence from the text.

> Emergency telephone numbers allow people to report fires quickly, and the sirens on firefighters' trucks smooth the way for a brigade to navigate around motorists efficiently and reach a fire within minutes.

What does the word <u>motorist</u> **most likely** mean?

Ⓐ a person who likes cars

Ⓑ a person who fights fires

Ⓒ a person who drives a car

Ⓓ a person who calls the fire department.

19 This question has two parts. First, answer part A. Then, answer part B.

Part A

What is the author's purpose for writing this text?

Ⓐ to explain fire safety tips

Ⓑ to describe the job of a firefighter

Ⓒ to describe how firefighters extinguish fires

Ⓓ to explain how firefighters protect themselves

Part B

Which detail from the text **best** supports your answer in part A?

Ⓐ "The most common cause of a fire in a house or apartment usually has something to do with cooking or heating."

Ⓑ "48.7% of residential fires were caused by cooking."

Ⓒ "People on the street below notice the haze, look up to see the dark smoke, and start to yell and wave their arms."

Ⓓ "Firefighters' other responsibilities include responding to emergency medical situations."

20 The author claims that firefighters must be dedicated to their jobs. Which of the following details from the text support the author's claim? Select **three** options.

Ⓐ "Many thousands of firefighters are injured every year while fighting fires or training for their jobs."

Ⓑ "For example, at the scene of a fire, some firefighters are overcome by heat exhaustion, or they strain their backs while handling fire hoses."

Ⓒ "The majority of firefighter injuries reported to the National Fire Incident Reporting System (NFIRS) are associated with residential fires."

Ⓓ "For example, firefighters may be called to a lakefront to assist in rescuing and reviving a drowning victim."

Ⓔ "Every year, advances lead to new and better types of firefighting equipment."

21 How does the author illustrate what happens when a fire is discovered? Include examples from the text to support your answer.

_____

_____

_____

_____

_____

Writing

Read and answer each question.

22 Jesse is writing a story for his class. He wants to revise it to eliminate any misspelled words. Read the conclusion from his story, and complete the task that follows.

> City life had always inspired Gregory—the bright lights, the bustling people, and tall buildings really excited him. As he entered the subway station, he heard a faint rythym reverberating through the underground tunnel. He smiled when he realized those sounds were coming from the subway platform where a young drummer was playing. Gregory watched him in awe, amazed at his talent. Beads of sweat framed his forehead as the drummer maintained a complicated beat. Gregory shook his head, smiling. Not once did the young man make a blunndar while he played. *How I love this city*, Gregory thought to himself.

Underline the **two** words that have spelling errors.

23 Choose the sentence that contains a spelling error.

Ⓐ In the winter, Elsie's mother always makes her favorite soup.

Ⓑ There are few things I enjoy more than visiting with good friends.

Ⓒ Gretchen ordinarily stays with her cousins during school vacations.

Ⓓ He tried to hoyst the backpack onto his shoulder, but it was too heavy.

24 Jamal is writing a story about visiting his grandmother. He wants to revise it to eliminate any fragments. Read the draft of one paragraph from his story, and complete the task that follows.

> My grandmother has a beautiful old grand piano that I love to play when I visit her. When I press the keys, a rich sound fills the house—from the living room to the upstairs bedroom. <u>My grandmother smiles when I play. Because she says it brings back old memories of when my mother was young.</u>

Which revision **best** corrects the underlined sentences?

Ⓐ My grandmother smiles when I play, she says it brings back old memories of when my mother was young.

Ⓑ My grandmother smiles when I play, so she says it brings back old memories of when my mother was young.

Ⓒ My grandmother smiles when I play, and because she says it brings back old memories of when my mother was young.

Ⓓ My grandmother smiles when I play, because she says it brings back old memories of when my mother was young.

25 Ming wrote a story about a girl who visited the Grand Canyon. Read the paragraph from her story, and complete the task that follows.

> Until Maria saw the Grand Canyon in person, she had no idea just how magnificent it was. The pictures Maria had seen didn't quite convey its sheer enormity or its splendor. Maria was also excited about visiting Lake Tahoe. Standing at the ledge, looking out at it, Maria couldn't speak—could barely breathe actually. The world could certainly be a beautiful and astonishing place. Later, Maria and her family had a wonderful picnic lunch.

Underline the **two** sentences that are not necessary to include in the paragraph.

26 Quentin is writing a passage about his first day of school. Read the draft of his first paragraph, and complete the task that follows.

> I arrived at my new school a half-hour early. I wanted to <u>see</u> the hallways and classrooms before class started, because I was afraid I would get lost. My new school was much bigger than my old school, so it would take some getting used to.

Quentin wants to replace the underlined word to make his meaning clearer. Which **two** phrases would be better choices?

Ⓐ acquaint myself with

Ⓑ quickly look at

Ⓒ run around

Ⓓ get away from

Ⓔ ignore completely

Ⓕ become familiar with

27 Which of the following sentences has an error?

Ⓐ I love to learn about many new things.

Ⓑ Melissa wants to be a writer when she grows up.

Ⓒ The meal we had for dinner was absolutely delicious.

Ⓓ The bumblebee foundation is a charity that was started by a nine-year-old.

28 Marilyn is writing a story about adventures in babysitting. She wants to revise it to eliminate any grammar errors. Read the draft of one paragraph from her story, and complete the task that follows.

> After we lured the cat down from the tree, we returned to the house and I collapsed onto the couch in utter exhaustion. Eddie played quietly at my feet, and I closed my eyes for just a moment. When I opened them, Eddie had vanished. I heard movement in the kitchen, so I dashed over to find that Eddie had stacked books and puzzles onto a kitchen chair and placed it against the fridge. He eyed his tower and moved to scale it to reach the cookies perched atop the fridge. <u>"Stop what you are doing before you get hurt?" I shouted to Eddie.</u>

Which revision **best** corrects the underlined sentence?

Ⓐ   "Stop what you are doing before you get hurt"? I shouted to Eddie.

Ⓑ   "Stop what you are doing before you get hurt!" I shouted to Eddie.

Ⓒ   "Stop what you are doing before you get hurt." I shouted to Eddie.

Ⓓ   "Stop what you are doing before you get hurt" I shouted to Eddie.

29 A student is writing a story about a day at the zoo. The student needs to use words that are precise and descriptive in her narrative. Read the paragraph from the draft of the story, and answer the question that follows.

> Yesterday was a <u>bad day</u> because I lost my little sister. It was Sophia's sixth birthday and she loves animals, so we went to the zoo. She loves to mimic the monkeys, laugh at the llamas, and <u>she likes</u> the polar bears.

Which set of words **best** replaces the underlined phrases with more precise and descriptive language?

Ⓐ   absolute disaster, peer at

Ⓑ   great time, play with

Ⓒ   not good, look at

Ⓓ   great adventure, poke

30 The following paragraph is from a writer's fictional narrative about a family that lives on Mars. It has errors in development and organization. Read the paragraph, and question that follows.

Mars is the fourth closest planet to the Sun. It is the seventh largest planet in the solar system. Most importantly, it will be our family's home for the next ten years. <u>My mother always wanted to join her father on the Red Planet, and last year she received the hologram message that changed our lives. It was Grandpa, and he was inviting us to come live with him on Mars! In 2050, humans first began to colonize Mars with the help of a brilliant astronaut and scientist. He just happens to be my grandfather.</u>

Which revision **best** organizes the underlined portion of the paragraph?

Ⓐ In 2050, humans first began to colonize Mars with the help of a brilliant astronaut and scientist. He just happens to be my grandfather. It was Grandpa, and he was inviting us to come live with him on Mars! My mother always wanted to join her father on the Red Planet, and last year she received the hologram message that changed our lives.

Ⓑ It was Grandpa, and he was inviting us to come live with him on Mars! My mother always wanted to join her father on the Red Planet, and last year she received the hologram message that changed our lives. In 2050, humans first began to colonize Mars with the help of a brilliant astronaut and scientist. He just happens to be my grandfather.

Ⓒ My mother always wanted to join her father on the Red Planet, and last year she received the hologram message that changed our lives. In 2050, humans first began to colonize Mars with the help of a brilliant astronaut and scientist. He just happens to be my grandfather. It was Grandpa, and he was inviting us to come live with him on Mars!

Ⓓ In 2050, humans first began to colonize Mars with the help of a brilliant astronaut and scientist. He just happens to be my grandfather. My mother always wanted to join her father on the Red Planet, and last year she received the hologram message that changed our lives. It was Grandpa, and he was inviting us to come live with him on Mars!

31 Mia wrote a story about getting stung by a jellyfish. Read the introduction to Mia's story, and complete the task that follows.

> I have always loved the ocean. My parents taught us how to swim at a very young age. One day I went for a swim and felt a bad sting. I didn't pay attention to it at first, but it started to really hurt. I got out of the water to find my parents. I showed them where the sting was. The area was already puffy.

Rewrite the paragraph to be more descriptive. Be sure to include vivid details and sensory words.

_____

_____

_____

_____

_____

Listening

Listen to the presentation. Then answer the questions.

The Great Thinker

32 Which detail from the presentation is an example of the experiments Newton did?

Ⓐ But Newton is most famous for his findings about gravity.

Ⓑ As a child, he was always thinking about experiments he wanted to perform.

Ⓒ He became the first person to prove that sunlight contains all the colors of the rainbow.

Ⓓ He tested and tried to improve each kite in order to determine which shape flew the best.

33 Which details from the presentation explain how Newton proved sunlight contains all the colors of the rainbow? Select **two** details.

Ⓐ In 1655, he spent a year experimenting.

Ⓑ Isaac Newton was born in England in 1642.

Ⓒ But Newton is most famous for his findings about gravity.

Ⓓ He did this by experimenting with a triangular piece of glass. . . .

Ⓔ When a beam of light passes through the prism, the light breaks apart into different colors. . . .

34 Which of the following are **two** ideas from the presentation?

Ⓐ Flying kites was Newton's favorite hobby.

Ⓑ Newton was the first person to create gravity.

Ⓒ Newton experimented with kites, prisms, and gravity.

Ⓓ Newton did not discover gravity when an apple fell to the ground.

Ⓔ Many of Newton's discoveries turned out to be myths.

Name _____ Date _____

Listen to the presentation. Then answer the questions.

Jackie Robinson—Breaking Barriers

Name _____ Date _____

35 Which details from the presentation support the idea that Jackie Robinson is an American hero? Select **two** details.

    Ⓐ He told him that he would have to ignore whatever abuse came his way.

    Ⓑ It was the first attempt to break the unwritten code of the color barrier in baseball.

    Ⓒ Robinson had been playing for the Kansas City Monarchs, a team of the Negro American League.

    Ⓓ Robinson knew that his example would help other African American players get a chance to play.

    Ⓔ When the National Association of Base Ball Players was formed in 1867, it banned African American players.

36 Which of the following is an idea from the presentation?

    Ⓐ Branch Rickey was known as an American hero.

    Ⓑ Baseball was one of many segregated sports in the 1940s.

    Ⓒ Some people did not want Jackie Robinson to play baseball.

    Ⓓ The Brooklyn Dodgers is the greatest baseball team in history.

37 This question has two parts. First, answer part A. Then, answer part B.

Part A

Which of the following is a key idea from the presentation?

    Ⓐ Jackie Robinson was an African American baseball player.

    Ⓑ Jackie Robinson played for two different baseball teams.

    Ⓒ Branch Rickey also worked as a scout for the Brooklyn Dodgers.

    Ⓓ Branch Rickey was also important to breaking the color barrier in baseball.

Part B

Which detail from the presentation **best** supports your answer in part A?

    Ⓐ Branch Rickey . . . saw him play.

    Ⓑ Branch Rickey . . . approached him about playing for the Dodgers.

    Ⓒ On that day, Robinson stepped onto the field in a Brooklyn Dodgers uniform.

    Ⓓ Today, Jackie Robinson is remembered as one of America's heroes, having changed our country for the better.

Name _____ Date _____

Listen to the presentation. Then answer the questions.

Saving Our Rivers

Name _____ Date _____

38 This question has two parts. First, answer part A. Then, answer part B.

Part A

Which of the following is a key idea in the presentation?

Ⓐ America's rivers are in trouble.

Ⓑ America's rivers are used to help make energy.

Ⓒ The American Rivers organization started the National River Cleanup in 1991.

Ⓓ Over a million volunteers have eliminated more than twenty million pounds of litter from rivers.

Part B

Which detail from the presentation **best** supports your answer in part A?

Ⓐ They are also are used for irrigation and the production of energy.

Ⓑ When river savers roll up their sleeves and get to work, the results can be impressive!

Ⓒ These waterways often play a role in a community's economy because of the recreational activities they support.

Ⓓ Only 21 percent of our rivers are described by the Environmental Protection Agency (EPA) as "healthy biological communities" able to sustain life.

39 Which detail from the presentation supports the idea that rivers are the lifeblood of a region?

Ⓐ They are an important source of drinking water.

Ⓑ Keeping them clean and safe is a goal everyone should share.

Ⓒ When river savers roll up their sleeves and get to work, the results can be impressive!

Ⓓ Over half of them are unable to support the fish and vegetation that are important parts of the river ecosystem.

40 Which of the following is an idea from the presentation?

Ⓐ It is safe to drink from most rivers.

Ⓑ Rivers are safe places for wildlife to live.

Ⓒ People should care about the health of their rivers.

Ⓓ The Environmental Protection Agency supports recreational activities on rivers.

Name _____ Date _____

Research

Read and answer each question.

41 Rodriguez is researching the history of space exploration and found this diagram.

Memorable Moments in Space Exploration	
October 4, 1957 *Sputnik 1* • first satellite ever launched • beginning of space age • signal of Russia's technical leadership	April 12, 1961 *Vostok 1* • first spacecraft to launch with a human • cosmonaut Yuri A. Gagarin first human in space • Gagarin traveled one orbit around Earth
July 20, 1969 *Apollo 11* • first humans on the moon • astronaut Neil Armstrong commanded the *Apollo 11* • Armstrong's famous words: "That's one small step for man, one giant leap for mankind."	April 24, 1990 Hubble Space Telescope • most sophisticated telescope to orbit Earth • photographs that it took forever changed field of astronomy • placed into orbit by astronauts on the space shuttle *Discovery*
June 21, 2004 *SpaceShipOne* • first private vehicle to fly past boundary of space • manned by Mike Melvill, first commercial astronaut-pilot • designed by Scaled Composites	

What information can Rodriguez learn from the diagram? Choose **two** answers.

Ⓐ how space travel developed over the years

Ⓑ why Russia is the leader in space travel today

Ⓒ when important events in space history occurred

Ⓓ where astronauts would like to travel in the future

Ⓔ who are the least well-known astronauts in space history

Ⓕ what the pictures from the Hubble Space Telescope looked like

42 A student is researching cloud formation and found the diagram below. Look at the diagram. Circle the **three** clouds that form at the lowest levels.

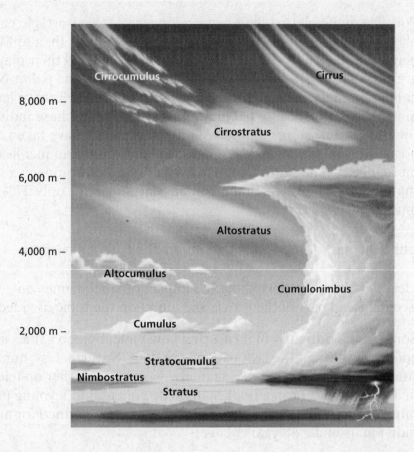

43 Oscar is writing a report on the life of Harriet Tubman. He came across several sources written by authors who had a variety of purposes for writing. Which of the following would be **most** useful for Oscar to use as he gathers his research?

Ⓐ an author whose purpose is to show readers Harriet Tubman's life in comic strips

Ⓑ an author whose purpose is to persuade readers that Harriet Tubman's life was lonely

Ⓒ an author whose purpose is to inform readers of the facts about Harriet Tubman's life

Ⓓ an author whose purpose is to entertain readers with fictional accounts of Harriet Tubman's life

Name _____ Date _____

44 A student is researching the music industry for a report she is writing. Read the part of the article she found on the topic of MP3s.

Portable audio players have come a long way, from portable cassette players in the 1970s, to CD players in the 1990s, and then to MP3 players in the 2000s. While the benefits of MP3s and their players are clear—listeners can hold thousands of songs in the palms of their hands—we must not discount the negative effect MP3s have had on the music industry. Because people can more easily purchase individual songs on online stores that sell MP3s, album sales have taken a nosedive. The advent of MP3s has also been tied to an increase in music piracy. The NPD Group, a market research company, estimates that in 2009 consumers in the United States paid for only 37% of their music.

Underline the part of the article that shows the author's purpose.

45 A student is writing a report about the impact of video games on adolescents. Read part of the article she found on the topic of video games.

Some of the difficulty in measuring how violent video games affect adolescents lies in the lack of concrete data. Nevertheless, numerous studies have shown that taking in any violence, whether on television, in a video game, or in a book, can be detrimental to a young person's mind. As a result, violent video games should be banned for all individuals under 18 years of age.

Which **two** answers explain the author's purposes for writing the article?

Ⓐ The author wrote the article to persuade readers to ban violent video games.

Ⓑ The author wrote the article to teach readers how to play violent video games.

Ⓒ The author wrote the article to entertain readers with stories about violent video games.

Ⓓ The author wrote the article to inform readers about the dangers of violent video games.

Ⓔ The author wrote the article to provide readers with reasons why violent video games are harmless.

Ⓕ The author wrote the article to promote a new violent video game that is popular among adolescents.

Performance Task 1
Part 1

Vikings

Task:

Your class has decided to focus on ancient cultures as a class project. You become interested in learning more about Vikings. You have found three sources about this topic in the school library.

After you have reviewed these sources, you will answer some questions about them. Briefly scan the sources and the three questions that follow. Then, go back and read the sources carefully so you will have the information you need to answer the questions and complete your research. You may use scratch paper to take notes on the information you find in the sources as you read.

In Part 2, you will write a story on a topic related to the sources.

Directions for Beginning:

You will now examine several sources. You can reexamine any of the sources as often as you like.

Research Questions:

After reviewing the sources, use the rest of the time in Part 1 to answer three questions about them. Your answers to these questions will be scored. Also, your answers will help you think about the information you have read, which should help you write your narrative.

You may refer back to your scratch paper to review your notes when you think it would be helpful. Answer the questions in the spaces below the items.

Your written notes on scratch paper will be available to you in Part 1 and Part 2 of the performance task.

Name _____ Date _____

Source #1

You have found an article that describes the characteristics of Vikings.

The Vikings: Raiders and Explorers

To many people, they were the Norsemen, "the men from the North." To those who had reason to fear them, they were the sea wolves. This image of the Vikings as ruthless raiders has been passed on for centuries.

The Vikings were also explorers and the first Europeans to reach America. Almost 500 years before Christopher Columbus set sail, the Vikings had already landed in the New World. They even built a settlement.

The Vikings lived in an area that includes the present-day countries of Norway, Sweden, and Denmark. In those days, the Vikings weren't known as Vikings. They weren't given that name until long after the Viking Age had ended.

The Scandinavian climate was typical of northern regions. It had long winters and short summers. This made farming a challenge. Most of the people lived along the coastline, where the warmer ocean waters created a milder winter. The Vikings used the sea as a means of transportation and a source of food. Most Vikings, however, were farmers who spent their time working the land.

From the beginning, Scandinavia's climate and geography were key factors that led the Vikings to explore new lands. Food, in fact, was the biggest motivator. The Vikings did the best they could with what they had. They ate seafood and raised dairy cattle, pigs, chickens, ducks, and sheep. However, the long, cold winters, the short growing season, and a lack of good farmland made it difficult to provide enough food for everyone. The farmers' main crops were only onions, leeks, peas, and cabbage. To make matters worse, the Viking population was growing, and so there were more mouths to feed.

Finding new lands on which to settle some of their people was one way to solve this problem. The Vikings raided anywhere their ships could reach. They took what they wanted and often killed the rightful owners.

Viking warriors were fierce fighters, especially if there was something to be gained, such as control of a land rich with resources. For almost 300 years, Viking warships and raiders seemed to be nearly everywhere. The Vikings probably first raided along the coast of Europe. Then they headed inland into Germany, France, and Spain. They even sailed along the Mediterranean Sea into Italy.

Their ships also crossed the North Sea and headed west to the British Isles. They stormed England, Scotland, Ireland, and the smaller islands clustered around them. They even reached farther eastward into what is now Russia. Some Vikings went into what is now Turkey. Some made it to what is now Iraq.

Though their voyages usually involved raids, the Vikings also visited trading centers. When they saw something they wanted, they would trade their own products. These included fur, lumber, and handcrafted objects. The Vikings also traded goods they had stolen in various raids. Sometimes they paid for the goods they wanted with silver coins. Some of what they bought were necessities they did not have at home. They also bought luxury goods such as silver, glassware, pottery, silk, and spices.

The arrival of the Vikings in North America seems to have resulted from a series of accidental discoveries made by Viking adventurers. Step by step, these smaller discoveries brought the Vikings closer and closer to their biggest discovery of all—the continent of North America.

The Vikings' first step toward North America was their discovery and settling of Iceland. Iceland would become the jumping-off point for Greenland. Greenland would become the stepping-stone to North America.

Source #2

You have found an article that focuses on the debate about whether Vikings actually settled in the New World.

The Vikings: The First Settlers in North America

For many years, scientists debated whether Vikings really came to North America. Those who thought so relied on Viking tales, called *sagas*, for proof. The Vikings didn't write down their history, but they did tell stories about their heroes and their adventures. The tales were finally written down in Iceland around the year 1200. This was a period when things were not going well for the Vikings. The writers may have felt that if people could read about the heroes of the Vikings' "golden age," it would help them get through the bad times.

The sagas give readers clues as to what Scandinavian society was like in those times. They provide information about the people the Vikings met, fought, and traded with. But they are stories, not factual evidence. They can't be counted on as absolute proof.

Name _____ Date _____

Hardworking archaeologists found more solid evidence using new scientific techniques. Archaeologists learn about human history by studying the places people lived and the artifacts they find. Artifacts are the things people leave behind that have survived into the modern era. Helge Ingstad was a writer and an adventurer. His wife, Anne Stine, was an archaeologist. The couple was sure that they could find the place the Vikings called Vinland along the coast of North America. They wanted to prove that the Vikings really did come to North America and that they did it about 500 years before Christopher Columbus or any other European.

In the 1960s, Ingstad began exploring Newfoundland, a large island just off the eastern coast of Canada. He looked for traces of ancient settlements. He also questioned the people living in the areas he was exploring. One question he always asked was "Have you seen any strange ruins in the area?" In a village on the north coast of Newfoundland, he finally got the answer he'd been waiting for. "Yes, follow me," said a fisherman named George Decker.

Decker led Ingstad to a site with a lot of grass and a small creek. This kind of place would make good pastureland for Viking farmers. More importantly, though, there were a number of mounds in the tall grasses. Ingstad quickly recognized them as the remains of ancient buildings. The fisherman thought American Indians may have left the buildings, but Ingstad believed they were built by Vikings. He set out to prove it.

The next step was an excavation to unearth the remains of the houses. Anne Stine led the excavation. Soon both believed that the buildings were longhouses resembling those the Vikings had lived in in Scandinavia. The diggers also found artifacts, such as nails and other objects. These suggested the Vikings had been repairing their boats on land.

Modern scientists have many ways of dating artifacts. In this case, they were able to date the wood found at the site using the science of studying tree rings. They discovered that the wood dated back to the time of Leif Erikson. Erikson had been identified as the first Viking to visit North America around the year 1000. So, there was certainly evidence to show that Vikings had lived at the site of the excavation.

But was this the spot where Leif himself landed? How long did the Vikings stay there? What did they do for recreational activities? And why did the Vikings leave? Maybe it was because of their many battles with unfriendly natives. Or it could be that the climate turned out to be colder than the Viking settlers expected, and they couldn't grow enough food for everyone.

Nobody really knows the answers to these questions. We also don't know where the Vikings went after they left Newfoundland. They may have returned to Iceland or to Scandinavia.

Name _____ Date _____

Still, the Vikings did have a great influence on those who came after them. Some historians believe that European explorers, like Columbus, who sailed in the fifteenth century, were encouraged to explore the West by reports of the Vikings' travels.

Source #3

You have found an article that discusses a specific archaeological find—a Viking ship! The article describes what the ship tells us about the way Vikings lived.

The Mystery of the Viking Ship

How did the Vikings travel so far over water? The answer was found in a large burial mound on the Gokstad farm outside of Sandefjord, Norway, in Scandinavia. Rumors had been circulating around the town that a Viking ship was buried deep in the mound. The location of the site made sense. Vikings in Norway were mostly farmers and the land in the area was a rich farming area.

One day, in 1879, two teen boys who lived on the Gokstad farm began to dig in the mound to see what they could find. There was the Viking ship! Nicolay Nicolysen, an antiquarian, or expert in ancient objects, heard about what the boys found. He stopped them from digging any farther and started an archaeological dig on the site.

The burial mound was about 16 feet high but had probably been even larger during the Viking period. As the archaeologists dug farther, they found that some of the upper part of the ship had been destroyed, but most of it was buried in clay below ground and had been preserved.

The dig revealed that most of the ship was made from oak, a wood that is hard and stable. The upper parts of the ship, the planks on the deck, and the mast were made of pine. Iron nails held the planks together. A keel, a T-shaped piece of wood that ran along the length of the boat, was attached to curved wooden planks, called *strakes*, in its center. These strakes acted as the ribs of the ship. Viking workers had overlapped the strakes. This was a method called *clinkering*. It made the ship strong. This ensured that the ship would be stable in rough seas and in battle.

But how did the ship travel in the sea? The dig revealed that there were places for 32 oarsmen to row, propelling the ship across the sea. A mast provided evidence that sails also helped the ship move. White cloth made of wool with red strips sewn on was found at the front of the ship. This was probably part of a sail. It suggested that harnessing the wind helped make the ship move.

The dig revealed clues about the structure of Viking ships. It also indicated some of the customs and rituals of the Viking people. There was a burial chamber at the back of the ship. The archaeologists found several revealing items. Between the joists on the roof, they found pieces of silk woven with gold thread, likely the remains of costly hangings. The hangings might have hung on the walls of the room in the stern.

One of the most important finds of all was a skeleton, which had been laid on a raised bed. The skeleton was probably a man of about six feet tall with a powerful build. Analysis of the skeleton indicated that he was likely in his forties when he died. On his legs was an indication that he had received blows, probably in battle. On the side of his thigh, there were signs of a deep knife wound. Archaeologists believe that this was the cause of death. This suggests that he died of a common fighting technique among the Vikings—a blow to the leg.

There were other items in the burial chamber. A game board and fish hooks were found. Kitchen equipment, 6 beds, a tent, 12 horses, 8 dogs, 2 peacocks, and 3 small boats were also discovered. All of these items tell us much about this man. He must have been rich to have owned so many items. Along with the skeleton, these items show us the ways that Vikings lived, fought, and died.

After the excavation, the ship was restored. Archaeologists took the ship apart and bent the parts that still existed into their original shape. They replaced the wood that had been destroyed with new wood. The ship stands in a museum in Sandefjord today.

When this Viking ship was in full sail, it must have been an impressive sight. The ship was incredibly useful to the Vikings. This well-designed vessel was stable and strong and able to navigate effectively in voyages of exploration, trade, and war. It was ultimately the burial site of what must have been a very powerful man.

40

1 In what way is the author's purpose for writing Source #2 similar to the author's purpose for writing Source #1? In what way is it different? Provide specific details to support your answer.

_____

_____

_____

_____

2 In which ways do Source #1 and Source #3 explain how Vikings lived? In your answer include at least **two** claims, **one** from each source that is supported with reasons and evidence.

_____

_____

_____

_____

3 Mark the boxes to match each source with the idea or ideas that it supports. Some ideas may have more than one source selected.

	Source #1: The Vikings: Raiders and Explorers	**Source #2:** The Vikings: The First Settlers in North America	**Source #3:** The Mystery of the Viking Ship
What role did Vikings play in history?			
What kind of evidence supports the idea that Vikings were the first to land in North America?			
What items in the burial chamber of the ship tell us how the Vikings lived?			

Part 2

You will now review your notes and sources, and plan, draft, revise, and edit your writing. You may use your notes and go back to the sources. Now read your assignment and the information about how your writing will be scored; then begin your work.

Your Assignment:

Your teacher wants each student to write a story about Vikings. You decide to write about a day in the life of a Viking. Your narrative will be read by other students and teachers.

In your story, you will write about a day in the life of a Viking who is going on a ship to explore North America. When writing your story, find ways to use information and details from the sources to improve your story. You could explain why you are leaving your home, describe what the ship looks like, and tell what happens when you land on the shore. Make sure you develop your character(s), the setting, and the plot, using details, dialogue, and description where appropriate.

REMEMBER: A well-written narrative
- contains an effective plot.
- develops a strong setting and characters.
- includes effective transitions.
- contains a logical sequence.
- includes an introduction and conclusion.
- develops characters, setting, experiences, and events.
- uses a variety of narrative techniques.
- contains effective sensory, concrete, and figurative language.
- uses correct sentence structure, punctuation, capitalization, grammar, and spelling.

Now begin work on your narrative. Manage your time carefully so that you can

1. plan your narrative.
2. write your narrative.
3. revise and edit the final draft of your narrative.

For Part 2, you are being asked to write a narrative that is several paragraphs long. Write your response on the following pages.

Remember to check your notes and your prewriting/planning as you write, and then revise and edit your informational article.

Name _____ Date _____

Name _____ Date _____

_____

_____

_____

_____

_____

_____

_____

_____

_____

_____

_____

_____

_____

_____

_____

_____

_____

_____

_____

_____

_____

_____

_____

_____

Name _____ Date _____

_____

_____

_____

_____

_____

_____

_____

_____

_____

_____

_____

_____

_____

_____

_____

_____

_____

_____

_____

_____

_____

_____

_____

_____

Assessment 2
Reading

Read the text. Then answer the questions.

Cleopatra: The Last Pharaoh

Cleopatra's Greek ancestors founded the dynasty of the Ptolemies in Egypt in 323 BCE. They once controlled vast territories. However, over time, these lands came under Roman control. Egypt was still an independent country, but its power had diminished greatly.

In 51 BCE, when the pharaoh Ptolemy XII died, his 18-year-old daughter Cleopatra VII and her younger brother, Ptolemy XIII, became co-rulers of Egypt. Cleopatra would not only become one of the most famous names in Egyptian history, she would be the last pharaoh to rule the country.

Cleopatra had many traits that qualified her to be pharaoh. She was an intelligent and well-educated young woman who spoke several languages and was skilled in mathematics. She was also attractive, ambitious, and ruthless. She would do almost anything to increase her power.

Her brother Ptolemy XIII was also ambitious. Many palace leaders supported him because they felt he was easier to control than Cleopatra. Three years into their joint rule, Ptolemy drove Cleopatra into exile. However, she quickly raised an army and prepared to fight to regain the throne.

About this same time, the Roman leader Julius Caesar entered Egypt in pursuit of an enemy. Cleopatra decided that if she could get Caesar on her side, she could not only regain her throne, but she might even be able to help Egypt recapture some of its former territories.

Caesar eventually committed Roman troops to fight on Cleopatra's behalf. Ptolemy XIII drowned trying to escape from Caesar's army. Cleopatra then took steps to remain on the throne by forging an alliance with Caesar.

Cleopatra had bet the future of Egypt on her ties with Caesar. It turned out to be an unlucky choice when Caesar's enemies assassinated him a few years later. Cleopatra was in Rome at the time. Realizing she was in danger, she quietly returned to Egypt.

Shortly after Cleopatra's return, her brother Ptolemy XIV, who was ruling as the pharaoh, died, and Cleopatra reclaimed the throne, co-ruling with her infant son, Ptolemy XV Caesar. Many people believe that Cleopatra ordered her brother to be poisoned so that she could regain power.

Meanwhile in Rome, the triumvirate of Octavian, Mark Antony, and Lepidus had taken Caesar's place. Lepidus had little power, but Octavian and Mark Antony both wanted to be the sole ruler. Octavian was Caesar's adopted son and heir, but he was sickly. He stayed in Rome while Mark Antony, who had fought with Caesar, ruled the eastern provinces. Three years after Caesar's death, Mark Antony called Cleopatra to appear before him in Tarsus, in what is now southern Turkey. He asked her to swear her loyalty. She was delighted with the opportunity to try once again to increase her power through her ties with Rome. As a result of their meeting, Antony abandoned his military plans and followed her back to Egypt.

Called back to Rome to deal with political problems, Antony left Cleopatra in Egypt. In Rome, Antony married the sister of Octavian in order to improve his relationship with his co-ruler. Politics kept him in Rome for four years. When he finally returned to the eastern provinces, Antony sent for Cleopatra and asked her to marry him. When Octavian heard about Antony's marriage to Cleopatra, he was outraged at this insult to his sister and himself. Octavian declared war on Cleopatra.

In the Battle of Actium in 31 BCE, Octavian blockaded Cleopatra's and Antony's fleets off the coast of Greece. Cleopatra's fleet managed to escape with Antony onboard one of her ships. Antony's fleet, however, was forced to surrender.

Ultimately, Cleopatra and Antony's story ended tragically. Cleopatra wanted to sever ties with Antony, so she fooled him into believing that she was dead. Antony killed himself when he heard the news of her death. Soon after, Cleopatra realized that Octavian planned to treat her as a defeated captive. Cleopatra chose to die rather than face that disgrace, and she, too, killed herself. After her death, Egypt fell under Roman rule. The era of the pharaohs had come to an end.

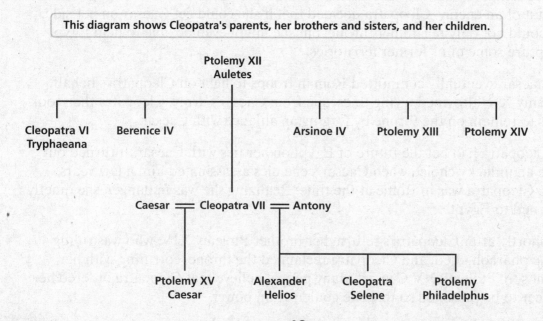

This diagram shows Cleopatra's parents, her brothers and sisters, and her children.

1 Read the sentence from the text.

> She was also attractive, ambitious, and <u>ruthless</u>.

Which of the following words have the same connotation as the word <u>ruthless</u>? Select **two** options.

- Ⓐ brutal
- Ⓑ challenging
- Ⓒ unmerciful
- Ⓓ compassionate
- Ⓔ violent

2 What topic in the text does the graphic **most** contribute to?

- Ⓐ Cleopatra's ancestors
- Ⓑ political events in Egypt
- Ⓒ the succession of the Roman leaders
- Ⓓ important events in Rome's history

3 Which of the following details from the text illustrates the idea that Cleopatra desired power?

- Ⓐ Cleopatra wanted to sever ties with Mark Antony.
- Ⓑ Ptolemy XIII was easier to control than Cleopatra.
- Ⓒ It is believed by many that Cleopatra poisoned her brother.
- Ⓓ Antony abandoned his military plans and followed Cleopatra back to Egypt.

4 Which of the following details supports the main idea that Cleopatra and Marc Antony's relationship was harmful to Egypt?

- Ⓐ Ptolemy drove Cleopatra into exile.
- Ⓑ Cleopatra was the last pharaoh to rule Egypt.
- Ⓒ Egypt fell under Roman rule after Cleopatra's death.
- Ⓓ Antony's fleet was forced to surrender to Octavian.

Name _____ Date _____

Read the text. Then answer the questions.

The Impact of Oil

In the past one hundred years, nothing has altered life in Alaska more than the discovery of large oil deposits in the state. Oil had been found in small amounts in Alaska before; the first Alaska wells were drilled on the Iniskin Peninsula back in 1898. But the development of the Prudhoe Bay oil fields in the 1960s changed everything.

In 1967, Richfield Oil was ready to leave the North Slope because it had drilled many dry holes. It decided to put forth one final effort before abandoning the area. The day after Christmas, part of the team opened up the rig to check the results of the most recent hole. Natural gas burst forth, and, when ignited with a small pipe in a high wind, it flared 50 feet. They hurried to create a second well to see if there was more gas and oil around it. In early 1968, the success of the other well was confirmed. They estimated that there were 9.6 billion recoverable barrels. That estimate has been increased to 13 billion.

This strike and others that came after it produced hundreds of thousands of barrels of oil per year. This made Alaska the second-largest oil-producing state in the United States. Texas, which represents a whopping 29% of the total United States oil output, is first.

For the people of Alaska, the discovery of oil meant thousands of good-paying jobs for geologists, drillers, and construction workers, to name a few. Geologists came to the region to explore the landscape and look for good drilling spots. Drillers came to sink wells into the ground and extract oil. Construction workers came to the North Slope. They built roads and housing as well as dining and medical facilities to serve oil field workers.

The discovery of oil has been a welcome boost to Alaska's economy. Earnings from the production and sale of oil gave workers money to burn! They spent it on a variety of things, including homes, food, education, and other basic needs. Also, the Alaskan government collects money from the oil companies, which averages $2 billion a year. The government uses this money to provide services to the people of Alaska and to limit their taxes.

But this discovery has also caused some problems. One of the most serious effects of the oil drilling is the damage it has done to the environment and to the culture of Alaska Natives.

Traditionally, Alaska Natives lived in family and village groups. They worked together and depended on each other. They hunted and fished on the land, traveling to find the game they needed. The arrival of the oil companies meant that land previously used by Alaska Natives would now be divided into areas owned by oil companies. Families and villages often split up as young people left their villages to work in the oil fields, leaving their traditional ways of life behind.

Oil drilling has harmed the environment, too. Road building and construction projects destroyed habitats used by caribou, bears, and other animals. Pollution from oil drilling tainted rivers, lakes, and streams. It killed fish and harmed wetlands. For thousands of years, Alaska Natives had depended upon game animals for food and clothing. Now these resources were vanishing.

Catastrophic oil spills further damaged the environment. In 1989, a huge oil tanker crashed on the rocks in Prince William Sound. It spilled more than 11 million gallons of oil along more than 1,000 miles of coastline. The oil spread over the waters like a black cloak, killing untold numbers of animals, including eagles, otters, loons, ducks, and fish. It hurt important fishing areas, including those used by Alaska Natives.

Cleanup began quickly. Even so, the massive spill overwhelmed the thousands of paid workers and volunteers. Courts ordered the oil company responsible for the spill to pay large fines to support the cleanup effort. It took twenty years before Prince William Sound was on its way to recovery, but the effects of the spill lingered on. Beaches still contained oil residue. Species such as the herring had not yet begun to recover.

The 1989 spill was not the only one. Hundreds of leaks from tankers, storage tanks, the Alaska Pipeline, and other sources occur each year. The spills contaminate wetlands and waterways. They threaten drinking water supplies. In many places, oil seepage will affect the environment for years to come.

Americans need the oil produced in Alaska, but it has eroded the cultural identity of the Alaska Natives and has contributed to the destruction of a once-pristine wilderness. In view of these consequences, this energy comes at a high cost.

Name _____ Date _____

5 Read the sentence from the text.

> Road building and <u>construction</u> projects destroyed habitats used by caribou, bears, and other animals.

What does the word <u>construction</u> **most likely** mean as it is used in the text?

Ⓐ full of constructing

Ⓑ similar to constructing

Ⓒ the process of constructing

Ⓓ the set of ideas about constructing

6 Which of the following is **most likely** the author's purpose for writing this text?

Ⓐ to persuade people that drilling for oil in Alaska should stop

Ⓑ to give information about the benefits and problems of drilling oil in Alaska

Ⓒ to explain how Alaska Natives have adapted to the changes brought by oil drilling

Ⓓ to convince people that the benefits of drilling oil in Alaska are greater than the problems

7 Read the sentence from the text.

> The oil spread over the waters <u>like a black cloak</u>, killing untold numbers of animals, including eagles, otters, loons, ducks, and fish.

What is the meaning of the phrase <u>like a black cloak</u> as it is used in the text?

Ⓐ It is a literal phrase describing a coat.

Ⓑ It is a figurative phrase telling how the oil looked.

Ⓒ It is a technical phrase relating to oil spills.

Ⓓ It is a lyrical phrase that adds rhythm.

Name _____ Date _____

8 Which of the following is a claim made in the text?

Ⓐ   Oil production in Alaska has harmed the environment.

Ⓑ   Oil is only found in small amounts in Alaska.

Ⓒ   Alaska Natives are against oil production.

Ⓓ   Alaska has only seen benefits from oil production.

Read the text. Then answer the questions.

The Eagle Has Landed

After several years of development and testing of new rockets and modules in the Apollo program, NASA set its sights on its ultimate goal: a man on the moon. To pilot the first moon mission, NASA chose some of the best pilots in the space program. Neil Armstrong had flown airplanes in the Korean War and spent hundreds of hours as a pilot testing flight equipment. Edwin "Buzz" Aldrin was also an airplane pilot who had graduated from military school and studied at one of the world's finest science colleges. The third, Michael Collins, had also graduated from military school and logged many hours as a test pilot. All had taken part in the earlier Gemini program. Together they would undertake the daring mission.

Apollo 11 launched on July 16, 1969. Around the world, millions of people watched the mission with wonder and joy. Thanks to technology, people could see the astronauts in action and listen in on their radio talks with NASA back on Earth.

It had been eight years since President John Kennedy had issued his moon mission challenge to the nation. Now *Apollo 11* would land the first humans on the moon.

It took four days to reach the moon. One hundred hours after starting their journey, Neil Armstrong and Buzz Aldrin entered the *Apollo 11* lunar module and began their descent to the moon's unfriendly surface. Michael Collins remained in the command module. Slowly and carefully, Armstrong and Aldrin steered the lunar module, which they called the *Eagle*. They guided the *Eagle* away from menacing boulders and set it down safely on the lunar surface. As millions of people on Earth watched and listened, Neil Armstrong made an announcement that thrilled people everywhere: "The *Eagle* has landed."

At NASA, the people in the mission control room cheered. About seven hours later, the astronauts were ready to take an even more important step— setting foot on the moon. Armstrong came out of the module first and set up a video camera to record his first steps. The whole world heard his words: "That's one small step for man, one giant leap for mankind."

After Armstrong, Buzz Aldrin also walked on the moon. Overall, they spent about twenty-one hours on the lunar surface. They collected rock samples to bring back to Earth for scientific experiments. Having finished that part of the mission, Armstrong and Aldrin prepared the lunar module to return to the command module. The crew back at NASA watched nervously, but the lunar module docked with the command module as planned. Soon, the three-man crew headed back to Earth, where they landed safely. The mission was a success!

After the first moon landing, five more Apollo flights landed on the moon. One other—*Apollo 13*—was forced to return to Earth after an in-flight emergency and did not complete its mission. Over the years, the Apollo astronauts explored the lunar surface further. They collected more samples from the moon and carried out many experiments.

Since the astronauts of *Apollo 17* left the surface of the moon in December 1972, no other human has visited it. Instead of more moon missions, NASA has explored space in other ways. It has sent reusable space shuttles to and from space stations. It has also sent unpiloted probes deep into space to collect data from other planets and objects in the solar system.

While we have learned a lot from these other missions, some people believe that it's time to visit the moon once again. Why go back to the moon? Perhaps the best reason is to build a permanent base there. A moon base would allow us to get a closer look at stars and other objects in our solar system. With a base on the moon, scientists could do experiments that may lead to the next great step into space: a mission to Mars with humans. Flying astronauts to the moon—or to Mars—would once again stretch the limits of technology. However, it would also pose risks to those on board and cost a great deal of money. These factors and many others will have to be weighed as we look toward the future of space exploration.

Name _____   Date _____

 Read the sentences from the text.

> One hundred hours after starting their journey, Neil Armstrong and Buzz Aldrin entered the *Apollo 11* lunar module and began their descent to the moon's unfriendly surface. Michael Collins remained in the command <u>module</u>.

What does the word <u>module</u> mean as it is used in the second sentence?

Ⓐ a part of a computer that does a certain job

Ⓑ a part of a space vehicle that can work alone

Ⓒ a self-contained, separated assembly of electronic parts

Ⓓ a set of parts that can be combined to build something

10 Which of the following events had to happen for the Apollo mission to be considered a success? Select **three** options.

Ⓐ launch of the rocket

Ⓑ landing of the *Eagle*

Ⓒ people listening to the radio talks

Ⓓ sending reusable space shuttles to space

Ⓔ lunar module docking with the command module

Name _____ Date _____

11 This question has two parts. First, answer part A. Then, answer part B.

Part A

What is the central idea of this text?

Ⓐ It is time to explore the moon again.

Ⓑ Space exploration is expensive and dangerous.

Ⓒ *Apollo 11* was the beginning of space exploration.

Ⓓ Apollo astronauts collected samples and carried out experiments.

Part B

Which detail from the text **best** supports your answer to part A?

Ⓐ After the first moon landing, five more Apollo flights landed on the moon.

Ⓑ However, it would also pose risks to those on board and cost a great deal of money.

Ⓒ A moon base would allow us get a closer look at stars and other objects in our solar system.

Ⓓ With a base on the moon, scientists could do experiments that may lead to the next great step into space: a mission to Mars with humans.

12 Read the sentence from the text.

They guided the *Eagle* away from <u>menacing</u> boulders and set it down safely on the lunar surface.

What does the word <u>menacing</u> mean as it is used in the text?

Ⓐ dangerous

Ⓑ oversized

Ⓒ flat

Ⓓ useless

Read the text. Then answer the questions.

Feeling the Heat

Scene 1

SETTING: a table in a busy lunchroom in Diven Middle School

Marvin: My palms get sweaty when I think about this assignment that Dr. Kellogg described today. I know we will learn a lot from doing our science experiment, but I'm super stressed, you guys!

Diego: [looking at science experiment websites on his tablet] Well, then, have I found the perfect experiment for us to do! Marvin, your sweaty palms could be the key to an A-plus for us!

Marvin and Ailaisha: [speaking in unison] What do you mean?

Diego: This experiment measures how stress affects our body temperatures. We will develop a hypothesis, conduct the experiment with ten volunteers, and then calculate the results to arrive at a conclusion that either proves or disproves our theory!

Marvin: Perfect, Diego! High-five sweaty palms!

Scene 2

SETTING: the next day in an empty classroom

Diego: Before we call in the first volunteers, let's review our plan. We have several different versions of a multiple-choice reading test. I'm so glad that Mr. Evans was able to give us some test items he used last year but wasn't using this year!

Ailaisha: He is the best English teacher! I'm just glad we didn't have to come up with the test ourselves.

Diego: Me too! So, the student needs to complete the test in just five minutes, and the score on the test needs to be above seventy percent for the person taking it to get a reward.

Marvin: What did we decide the reward was going to be? I forget!

Ailaisha: [holds up a giant plate of chocolate chip cookies covered with plastic wrap] Cookies!

Name _____ Date _____

Diego: Right, cookies. So, we have two basal thermometers and a stopwatch. Ailaisha, why don't you take over from here?

Ailaisha: Great. Thanks, Diego! I am going to bring in the people who have agreed to work as our subjects three at a time. We will first ask them to sit quietly for five minutes and then have them identify their level of stress on a scale of one to ten as I take their temperatures. Then, I am going to give them the tests and grade them while Marvin does his part. Take it away, Marvin!

Marvin: After the volunteers finish the test, I'll do the same thing Ailaisha did before they took the test. I will ask them to sit quietly for five minutes, record their stress levels, and also take their temperatures.

Diego: [claps his hands together] Awesome, everyone! Let's get this thing started!

Scene 3

SETTING: later in the day

Marvin: Did anyone notice that I was as cool as a cucumber during the entire experiment? There's nothing to be stressed about when you're working with a great team on a can't-fail experiment!

Ailaisha: I agree that the experiment went smoothly! Those volunteers were extremely cooperative. Hey, don't touch those cookies, Marvin! Those leftover cookies are going to be our reward when we ace our report!

Diego: Don't celebrate yet. While you have been chatting about inconsequential matters, I have been reviewing the data and plotting a preliminary graph with the stress-level numbers on the *x*-axis and the temperature measurements on the *y*-axis.

Ailaisha: If Marvin's sweaty palms were any indication, it should clearly show the relationship that we hope to establish.

Diego: According to our hypothesis, when I plot the data acquired from our experiment, we should observe the line going up and to the right to indicate a positive correlation between stress levels and temperature. In other words, as their stress increases, people's body temperatures should rise correspondingly.

Ailaisha: [frowns and furrows her brow] But the graph you drew shows the slope of the line going down! How is that possible?

Diego: I can't believe it either, but I have checked and rechecked the numbers. Our results clearly demonstrate a negative correlation, meaning the temperatures of our subjects decreased as their reported stress levels increased.

Marvin: There has to be a mistake! What could have happened to make our results so off from what we expected? [wiping his forehead and fanning himself] It doesn't make sense at all. We even did research before our experiment, and everything we read indicated the opposite should be true.

Ailaisha: Marvin, go sit at the testing table, and get ahold of yourself before you combust! Remember, Dr. Kellogg is always telling us to look for factors that can skew the outcome of an experiment. Did we have faulty equipment? Maybe Marvin and I took the subject's temperature differently, and so our measurements weren't right. Hey, Marvin, what's so funny!

Marvin: I think I might have found the factor that affected our results! This table is right below the air-conditioning vents. I was standing right behind the test-takers, so no wonder we all were able to keep our "cool"!

Diego: Unbelievable! I think we should repeat the experiment under better-controlled circumstances; that is, as soon as we bake more cookies. But when we report on the experiment, we should include what we learned from the first trial, too. After all, that's what experimentation is all about—trial and error!

---

13 Read the sentences from the text.

> **Diego:** Don't celebrate yet. While you have been chatting about <u>inconsequential</u> matters, I have been reviewing the data and plotting a preliminary graph with the stress-level numbers on the *x*-axis and the temperature measurements on the *y*-axis.

What is the **best** meaning of the word <u>inconsequential</u> as it is used in the text?

Ⓐ   wrongly significant

Ⓑ   across significant

Ⓒ   over significant

Ⓓ   not significant

14   This question has two parts. First, answer part A. Then, answer part B.

Part A

What is the theme of the text?

Ⓐ   Stay calm when faced with challenges.

Ⓑ   Careful planning always ensures success.

Ⓒ   Reward yourself after completing difficult tasks.

Ⓓ   Stressful situations lead to a rise in body temperature.

Part B

Which detail from the text **best** supports your answer to part A?

Ⓐ   Before we call in the first volunteers, let's review our plan.

Ⓑ   This experiment measures how stress affects our body temperatures.

Ⓒ   Those leftover cookies are going to be our reward when we ace our report!

Ⓓ   Marvin, go sit at the testing table, and get ahold of yourself before you combust!

Name _____ Date _____

15 Read the following lines from the text. Underline **one** sentence that creates a formal tone in the text.

> **Marvin:** Did anyone notice that I was as cool as a cucumber during the entire experiment? Maybe this experience has eradicated my stress reaction!

> **Ailaisha:** I agree that the experiment went smoothly! Those volunteers were extremely cooperative. Hey, don't touch those cookies, Marvin! Those leftover cookies are going to be our reward when we ace our report!

> **Diego:** Don't celebrate yet. While you have been chatting about inconsequential matters, I have been reviewing the data and plotting a preliminary graph with the stress-level numbers on the *x*-axis and the temperature measurements on the *y*-axis.

16 What causes Diego, Marvin, and Ailaisha to repeat their experiment? Include details from the text to support your answer.

_____

_____

_____

_____

Read the text. Then answer the questions.

Autobiography of a Dog

It was a warm and humid September evening in 1810 when I entered this
world. My birthplace was a cozy, straw-filled corner of the shed already occupied
by six brothers and sisters. I was the final pup. "Last but not least," Mr. Porter
said admiringly. "This one is going to beat them all in weight and height!" Before
too long, though, I was an only child. Mr. Porter gave my brothers and sisters to
other settlers in the valley, but because the children, Emma and George, begged
to keep me, I stayed with my ma on the farm. Together, Ma and I kept an eye
on those flighty chickens, apt to wander off, and the rambunctious cattle. We
made sure we protected our human flock as well. My favorite job was following
Emma and George to the Mississippi River when they went fishing. By the time
I finished splashing around trying to catch those leaping trout, we all looked as if
we had been swimming!

Not everyone appreciated my efforts, though. "Bo's kind of like a big wolf,
isn't he?" Grandma Sarey would say with a sniff, lifting her skirts out of the
way as if I might step on them or knock into her. "He sure takes up his share
of space." Those comments hurt my feelings. Mrs. Porter tried to make up for
them by giving me an extra pat on the head or slipping me a piece of buttermilk
biscuit, as if to say, "Don't you worry yourself. She'll get accustomed to you
sooner or later."

One night—December 16, 1811, to be precise—Ma and I were guarding the
henhouse. We had both been restless all day, sensing that something was wrong.
The night was so dark that it felt like we had black cloth sacks over our heads.
Suddenly, we were startled by a tremendous roaring noise like the rushing of a
huge waterfall right next to us. As we looked around, we heard thunder cracking
and saw lightning flashing—not from the sky, but from below us. Ma and I raced
toward the cabin to warn our humans just as the Porters and Grandma Sarey
came out in their nightclothes, yelling, "Earthquake!" Before I could figure
out what that word meant, the ground started heaving, buckling up and then
tumbling down as if a giant were stamping his foot. The surface of the Earth
splintered, and huge cracks appeared in it, swallowing enormous trees in one
gulp. While Mr. Porter yelled for Ma to help him round up the livestock, I barked
at the rest of the family to move closer to the henhouse.

Name _____ Date _____

Just then, Alice the cow cantered off in fright down the east field. Grandma Sarey took off after her. Giving a final bark to Mrs. Porter and the children to stay put, I crouched low to the ground and followed. Thick, stinging, wet smoke filled the air, making it almost impossible to track Grandma's scent. Then, in the distance, I heard Alice bawling and Grandma yelling at her to stop. Grandma's voice changed to a plea for help. Fear gave my paws wings, and I flew across the landscape, skimming the ground.

Finally, I stopped, listening carefully to try to hone in on Grandma's location. I found Alice trembling next to a deep, raw gully with Grandma Sarey at the bottom. I nosed my way down to the bottom of the slope, where Grandma threw her arms around me. I gently tugged her to her feet and backed my way out of the ravine, yanking her with me. At the top, Grandma took a breath. "Bo, I am so sorry I ever compared you to a wolf. Without you, I don't know what I would have done." My bark of joy sounded across the field, bringing Mr. Porter and Ma running. Together, all of us made our way back to the cabin, where Grandma insisted I come in for a big piece of bacon. "My hero!" she said, ruffling the top of my head.

---

17 Read the sentence from the text.

> Fear gave my paws wings, and I flew across the landscape, skimming the ground.

What does the phrase <u>fear gave my paws wings</u> **most likely** mean?

Ⓐ Bo is able to fly to save Alice and Grandma.

Ⓑ Bo runs faster when he hears Grandma's cry for help.

Ⓒ Bo is scared because he can't find Alice and Grandma.

Ⓓ Fear gives Bo wings to put on his paws to save Alice and Grandma.

Name _____ Date _____

18 Underline **two** sentences that show how Grandma's point of view changes.

Finally, I stopped, listening carefully to try to hone in on Grandma's location. I found Alice trembling next to a deep, raw gully with Grandma Sarey at the bottom. I nosed my way down to the bottom of the slope, where Grandma threw her arms around me. I gently tugged her to her feet and backed my way out of the ravine, yanking her with me. At the top, Grandma took a breath. "Bo, I am so sorry I ever compared you to a wolf. Without you, I don't know what I would have done." My bark of joy sounded across the field, bringing Mr. Porter and Ma running. Together, all of us made our way back to the cabin, where Grandma insisted I come in for a big piece of bacon. "My hero!" she said, ruffling the top of my head.

19 Which of the following details from the text explains why "Grandma's voice changed to a plea for help"?

Ⓐ Grandma Sarey took off after her.

Ⓑ Then, in the distance, I heard Alice bawling and Grandma yelling at her to stop.

Ⓒ I found Alice trembling next to a deep, raw gully with Grandma Sarey at the bottom.

Ⓓ Thick, stinging, wet smoke filled the air, making it almost impossible to track Grandma's scent.

20 What is the theme of the text? Include details from the text to support your answer.

_____

_____

_____

_____

21 How does Bo respond to danger in the text? Select **three** options.

Ⓐ He helps round up the livestock.

Ⓑ He keeps an eye on the chickens.

Ⓒ He runs to the cabin to warn people.

Ⓓ He pulls Grandma Sarey out of a ravine.

Ⓔ He barks at the family to get them to move closer to the henhouse.

Name _____ Date _____

Writing

Read and answer each question.

22 Marisa is writing a story for class. She wants to revise to eliminate any misspelled words. Read a paragraph from her story, and complete the task that follows.

> The young woman walked down the empty street late at night and shuderred as the wind whistled through the trees, reminding her to button up her coat tightly. Farther down under a lone streetlight, a man stood awaiting her arrival. She quickened her pace to meet him. When she arrived, he handed her an envelope. She seized it from his hands, and, forgetting even to say thank you, she briskly strode away.

Underline the **two** words that have spelling errors.

23 Choose the sentence that contains a spelling error.

Ⓐ When the truth was revealed, Luke learned the consequences of his actions.

Ⓑ Please retain your receipt in case you want to return your purchase.

Ⓒ Ms. Barrett wrote the math equations on the board before class started.

Ⓓ It was hard for her to consentrate on her homework because of the loud music playing.

24 Giovanni is writing a story about his favorite meal. He wants to revise to eliminate any errors. Read a paragraph from his story, and complete the task that follows.

> The second course was a pasta dish that was cooked to perfection. It had only three ingredients in addition to the pasta! <u>It had grilled shrimp drizzled with olive oil or red pepper flakes sprinkled over the top, and it wasn't too spicy.</u> It was just right.

What revision **best** fixes the underlined sentence?

Ⓐ It had grilled shrimp drizzled with olive oil, but red pepper flakes over the top, and it wasn't too spicy.

Ⓑ It had grilled shrimp drizzled with olive oil and red pepper flakes over the top, but it wasn't too spicy.

Ⓒ It had grilled shrimp drizzled with olive oil, red pepper flakes over the top, and it wasn't too spicy.

Ⓓ It had grilled shrimp drizzled with olive oil and red pepper flakes over the top, or it wasn't too spicy.

25 Pierre wrote a paragraph explaining why men should be given paternity leave. Read the paragraph and think about the changes he should make.

> It is very important for fathers to have time off when their baby is born, and so they should be given paternity leave. The baby needs to bond with both parents, not just the mother, who may be on maternity leave from work. In addition, taking care of a baby is hard work. It would be really helpful for the father to be at home to have both parents to help out. One of the hardest things to do is to bathe a new baby. Paternity leave should be offered to all fathers. Companies should not complain about maternity leave, because that should be a given.

Underline the **two** sentences that are not necessary to include in the paragraph.

Name _____ Date _____

26 Jared is writing an essay about why school sports should not lose funding. Read the draft of his first paragraph, and complete the task that follows.

> It would be a big mistake on the school's part to cut school sports funding. Being on a sports team gives students a ton of benefits—the biggest being that sports keep students active and healthy. However, there are many other positive <u>things</u> as well. For example, students learn how to work as a member of a team and to think of the group instead of just themselves. They also experience firsthand why it pays off to keep going. Lastly, they learn the importance of good sportsmanship.

Jared wants to replace the <u>underlined</u> word to make his meaning clearer. Which **three** words would be better choices?

Ⓐ results

Ⓑ ways

Ⓒ effects

Ⓓ thoughts

Ⓔ problems

Ⓕ outcomes

27 Which of the following sentences has an error in grammar usage?

Ⓐ The three of them took her own sweet time to get to the meeting.

Ⓑ Before Jennifer entered the gate, she got out her ticket.

Ⓒ As Mary prepared lunch, she hummed her favorite song.

Ⓓ Paul didn't want to lose his spot in line.

28 Which of the following sentences includes an indirect object?

Ⓐ The weather is cool, so wear a sweater.

Ⓑ The missing sock was in the laundry machine.

Ⓒ Adonis traded me three of his favorite baseball cards.

Ⓓ The painting was made in the late nineteenth century.

29 A student is writing a report about George Washington. The student needs to use words that are clear and specific in her report. Read the paragraph from the draft of the report, and answer the question that follows.

> George Washington's early childhood remains <u>a little bit of</u> a mystery. It is known that he spent <u>most</u> of it on the Ferry Farm in Virginia. In addition, his school papers reveal he studied mathematics, geography, and perhaps Latin. They also show he read some of the English classics, such as *The Spectator*.

Which set of words **best** replaces the <u>underlined</u> phrases with clearer and more-specific language?

Ⓐ small, some days

Ⓑ somewhat, time

Ⓒ partially, the majority

Ⓓ kind of, a good deal

30 Ricardo is writing a paper about albatrosses. Read the draft of a paragraph from his paper, and answer the question that follows.

> Albatrosses are large seabirds from the Diomedeidae family. They are similar to other oceanic birds in that they stay hydrated by drinking seawater. Although they have been known to feed on ships' garbage, they normally eat squid to survive. Albatrosses are <u>really terrific</u> gliders, and in windy weather they can glide for hours without ever having to use their wings.

Ricardo wants to replace the <u>underlined</u> phrase to make his meaning more exact. Which word would **best** make his word choice better?

Ⓐ good

Ⓑ average

Ⓒ impressive

Ⓓ better

Name _____ Date _____

31 Mendel is writing an informational paragraph about how to make French toast. The paragraph needs an introduction to the topic. Read the paragraph and directions that follow.

How to Make French Toast

First, gather the ingredients you will need: one egg, one teaspoon of vanilla extract, one quarter-cup of milk, and four slices of bread. Next, lightly grease a pan with butter or nonstick spray. Then, beat the egg and vanilla vigorously together in a bowl. Add the milk to the same bowl and mix again. Finally, dip the bread in the liquid mixture, taking care to coat both sides of the bread. Cook the bread slices in the coated pan on medium heat, flipping with a spatula once to be sure both sides are sufficiently browned. Place the finished French toast on a plate and enjoy!

Write text that could be added to the beginning of the paragraph to introduce the topic.

_____

_____

_____

_____

_____

Name _____ Date _____

Listening

Listen to the presentation. Then answer the questions.

Life under the Han Dynasty

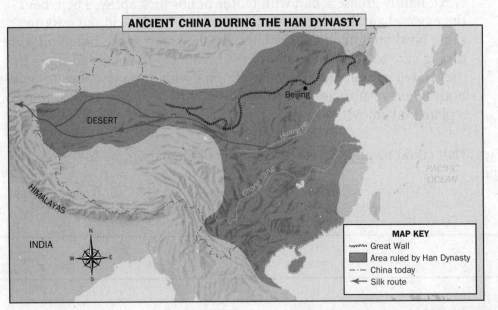

ANCIENT CHINA DURING THE HAN DYNASTY

MAP KEY
- Great Wall
- Area ruled by Han Dynasty
- China today
- Silk route

Name _____ Date _____

32 What is the purpose of the presentation?

Ⓐ to describe how farmers during the Han dynasty raised crops

Ⓑ to explain who made sandals and wove silk during the Han dynasty

Ⓒ to give information about farmers and ordinary people during the Han dynasty

Ⓓ to persuade people that life was easy for everyone during the Han dynasty

33 Which of the following are ideas from the presentation? Select **two** options.

Ⓐ People's lives improved under the Han dynasty.

Ⓑ The Han dynasty was successful but short-lived.

Ⓒ The demands on the people under the Han dynasty were severe.

Ⓓ Farmers were expected to leave their farms and serve in the military.

Ⓔ Men, women, and children contributed to the household in different ways.

34 Draw an X in each box to show which expectations applied to men, women, and children.

	Men	**Women**	**Children**
practice archery			
bring silk to market			
repair animal pens			
watch over animals			

73

Name _____ Date _____

Listen to the presentation. Then answer the questions.

What Pompeii Can Tell Us

35 What is the presentation **mostly** about?

Ⓐ Scientists matched foods they found in Pompeii to the recipes in a cookbook.

Ⓑ A university initiated a project to explore the ancient Roman city of Pompeii.

Ⓒ Recipes from a Roman named Apicius were collected and put in an ancient Roman cookbook.

Ⓓ The work of students, as well as the artifacts they found, helped scientists learn more about ancient Rome.

36 Which of the following is a key point from the presentation?

Ⓐ Workers were unable to find any new artifacts.

Ⓑ Workers had to be cautious when cleaning artifacts.

Ⓒ Workers had to search for artifacts without using any tools.

Ⓓ Workers found a cookbook when looking for artifacts.

37 This question has two parts. First, answer part A. Then, answer part B.

Part A

What is the purpose of this presentation?

Ⓐ to describe a typical meal the people of Pompeii ate

Ⓑ to persuade people to use an ancient Roman cookbook to make a typical Roman meal

Ⓒ to give information about how artifacts helped scientists identify what the people of Pompeii ate

Ⓓ to explain how workers and scientists found the recipes of a Roman named Apicius

Part B

Which of the following statements **best** supports the answer in part A?

Ⓐ They found traces of a wide range of foods.

Ⓑ Then scientists looked at the recipes from a Roman named Apicius.

Ⓒ They found many recipes for foods that might have been made in the gourmet kitchen of a wealthy family.

Ⓓ Scientists at Pompeii looked over the list of foods found in the area and matched them to the cookbook.

Name _____ Date _____

Listen to the presentation. Then answer the questions.

The Navajos

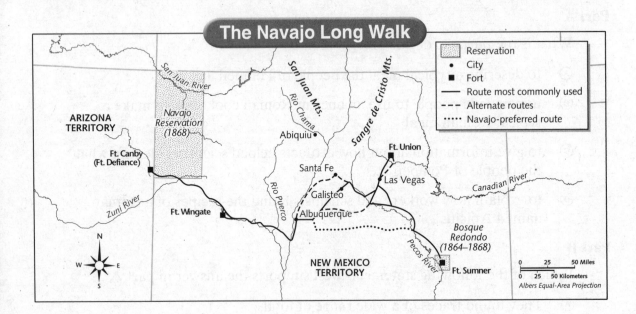

The Navajo Long Walk

38 What is the purpose of the presentation?

Ⓐ to tell a story

Ⓑ to teach a lesson

Ⓒ to give information

Ⓓ to persuade the reader

39 What is a central idea of the presentation?

Ⓐ The Navajos were originally hunters and farmers.

Ⓑ The Navajos were known for keeping large flocks of birds.

Ⓒ The Navajos raided other settlements for land as their primary goal.

Ⓓ The Navajos settled in Colorado but were forced out by the United States government.

40 Which of the following are key points in the presentation? Select **three** options.

Ⓐ The Navajos lived in clans.

Ⓑ Thousands died of starvation and disease on the reservation.

Ⓒ Hogans were structures framed with poles and covered with earth.

Ⓓ The Navajos raided other settlements, particularly those of the Spanish.

Ⓔ In 1863, the United States government forced the Navajos to move to a new settlement.

Name _____ Date _____

Research

Read and answer each question.

41 Patrice is researching an article on the human brain and found this diagram. What information can she learn from it? Choose **two** answers.

The Human Brain's Functional Areas

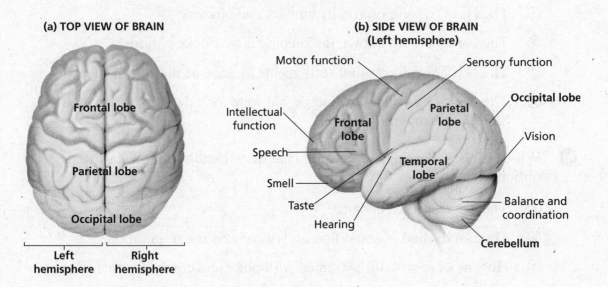

(a) TOP VIEW OF BRAIN

Frontal lobe
Parietal lobe
Occipital lobe

Left hemisphere   Right hemisphere

(b) SIDE VIEW OF BRAIN
(Left hemisphere)

Motor function   Sensory function
Intellectual function   Occipital lobe
Frontal lobe   Parietal lobe
Speech   Vision
Smell   Temporal lobe
Taste   Balance and coordination
Hearing   Cerebellum

Ⓐ the areas of the brain that control balance and coordination

Ⓑ the types of tissue that make up the human brain

Ⓒ the difference between the types of lobes

Ⓓ the definition of intellectual function

Ⓔ the part of the brain that allows humans to grow

Ⓕ the number of lobes in the human brain

42 A student is researching dental health and came across this advertisement for Brushaway toothpaste. Read the paragraph and underline **three** claims that support the main argument made in the text.

Maintaining dental health is very important. To ensure your teeth and gums stay healthy, use Brushaway toothpaste. Brushaway toothpaste contains a special ingredient that helps rid your teeth of unwanted plaque. With everyday use, Brushaway toothpaste will also keep your teeth their natural bright white color. No one wants to walk around with stained teeth. Moreover, Brushaway's special combination of ingredients makes your breath fresh. So keep using Brushaway and you'll keep smiling!

43 Keith is researching a paper on the country of Cambodia and finds the following text.

The young Cambodian woman bent down to touch the crumbling earth. Never had she lived through such an extreme drought. "If it doesn't rain soon," she thought to herself, "our crops will never survive." As she looked up at the sky, the sun shone brightly in her eyes, causing her to squint. The stark blue sky, which used to be so beautiful to her, now seemed to be her worst enemy.

What is the author's main purpose for writing this text?

Ⓐ to persuade

Ⓑ to inform

Ⓒ to entertain

Ⓓ to teach

Name _____ Date _____

44 A student is gathering data on the lifecycle of a housefly and found this diagram. What information can she learn from the diagram? Choose **three** answers.

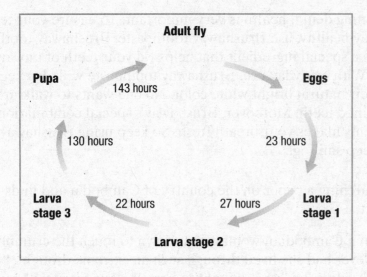

Ⓐ There are six stages in a fly's life cycle.

Ⓑ A fly spends the shortest time in larva stage 2.

Ⓒ Larvae go through three stages of development.

Ⓓ People sometimes mistake larvae for very tiny snakes.

Ⓔ Every fly lays twelve eggs during its reproductive cycle.

Ⓕ The scientific name for a fully formed housefly is *pupa*.

45 A student is gathering information about the author's purpose for writing. Look at the table she made. Circle the author's purpose for writing each of the three pieces of writing.

Type of Writing	Author's Purpose for Writing		
1. Folktale about a talking dog	to persuade	to inform	to entertain
2. Encyclopedia entry about giraffes	to persuade	to inform	to entertain
3. Magazine editorial, "Why Cell Phones Should Be Banned from School"	to persuade	to inform	to entertain

Name _____ Date _____

Performance Task 2
Part 1

The Fight for Civil Rights

Task:

Your school is making a website to highlight pieces of history from the twentieth century. You are interested in civil rights in the twentieth century and want to learn more about the events during that time. You have found three sources about this topic in the school library.

After you have reviewed these sources, you will answer some questions about them. Briefly scan the sources and the three questions that follow. Then, go back and read the sources carefully so you will have the information you will need to answer the questions and complete your research. You may use scratch paper to take notes on the information you find in the sources as you read.

In Part 2, you will write an informational article using information you have read.

Directions for Beginning:

You will now examine several sources. You can reexamine any of the sources as often as you like.

Research Questions:

After reviewing the research sources, use the rest of the time in Part 1 to answer three questions about them. Your answers to these questions will be scored. Also, your answers will help you think about the information you have read, which should help you write your informational article.

You may refer back to your scratch paper to review your notes when you think it would be helpful. Answer the questions in the spaces below the items.

Your written notes on scratch paper will be available to you in Part 1 and Part 2 of the performance task.

Name _____   Date _____

Source #1

You have found a source that discusses John Lewis and his contributions to civil rights.

John Lewis

When John Lewis was growing up, he had no idea that he would make an important contribution to the fight for civil rights, yet his name is remembered for the courage he has shown for fighting inequality.

John Lewis was born in 1940 on a small farm in rural Alabama. His family raised crops, including cotton and peanuts, as well as livestock. They worked from sunrise to sunset. Even so, there were times when they barely had enough food. There were other times when the children had to stay home to help with the harvest or the other work on the farm. John loved school and hated having to miss it. He occasionally hid under the front porch so he could run to the school bus. Then John would be on his way before anyone noticed that he wasn't at home! This passion for education led him to American Baptist College in Nashville. It was there that he studied to become a minister. He spent four years there. Then he continued for two more years at Fisk University. This is where his life changed. He came to know Dr. Martin Luther King Jr. and many other religious and social leaders. They were all working against laws that held African Americans back.

As an African American in the rural South, John Lewis had been exposed early to the segregation that put limits on the lives of him, his family, and his friends. He could not get a library card because the library was for whites only. He had to sit in the balcony in the small theater in his town of Troy. The seats downstairs were reserved for white children. His family had to pack food for their trip to visit their uncle in Buffalo, New York. This was because African Americans were not allowed in the restaurants along southern highways. In Buffalo, African Americans and whites attended the same schools, shopped in the same stores, and sat together in theaters. Everyone could use the same drinking fountain. This was different from the south, where the fountains were labeled "Whites Only" and "Colored."

This experience in Buffalo and his growing awareness of the struggle for civil rights led Lewis to believe that he had to help bring about an end to segregation. He realized how he could help make this happen while studying at Fisk. He and other students joined together to form the Student Nonviolent Coordinating Committee, or SNCC. By the time he was chosen to be chairman of the SNCC in 1963, Lewis had participated in many protests. He had also been arrested more than 20 times for violating laws he thought were unfair. In his role as chairman, he was asked to speak at a major civil rights event called the March on Washington. This event was held on August 28, 1963. There were estimated to be

Name _____ Date _____

hundreds of thousands of people in the crowd. John Lewis stood in front of them, and he spoke these words: "To those who have said, 'Be patient and wait,' we must say that 'patience' is a dirty and nasty word. We cannot be patient, we do not want to be free gradually. We want our freedom, and we want it *now*."

John Lewis went on to participate in many more protests, including the march from Selma to Montgomery in 1965. This demonstration, in which Alabama police attacked the marchers, brought attention to the restrictions that often prevented African Americans from exercising their right to vote.

Since then, Lewis has continued to work for justice. He first headed an agency dedicated to voter education and another that coordinated volunteers for the federal government. He then entered the political arena, winning a seat on the Atlanta City Council in 1981. From there, he went on to win a seat in the U.S. House of Representatives in 1986. He has been reelected in every election since then.

Source #2

You have found an article that discusses the events that caused an escalation in the civil rights movement.

Civil Rights for All

In Montgomery, Alabama, in 1955, an African American woman refused to give up her seat to a white man on the bus. Her name was Rosa Parks, and she was a member of the Montgomery branch of the National Association for the Advancement of Colored People (NAACP). She believed in civil rights and didn't move as a protest against the segregation laws of the time. Her action caused a bus boycott. African Americans refused to ride buses altogether during this boycott. This ultimately led to a Supreme Court order in 1956 to desegregate (end racial separation in) the bus system.

In Greensboro, North Carolina, in 1960, four black college students staged a demonstration by sitting at an all-white lunch counter. Their actions led college students all over the South to demonstrate in the same way.

Next came the Freedom Rides of 1961. This was to protest the separation of black and white people in bus terminals. Groups of white and black protestors went to bus stations. They did things like eat together at "white only" lunch counters and use "white only" restrooms.

All of these events signaled a rise in the civil rights movement. They also proved that the methods of nonviolent resistance that Dr. Martin Luther King Jr. supported could work to bring about political change.

Nowhere was this more visible than on the Mall in front of the Lincoln Memorial in Washington, D.C., on August 28, 1963. The March on Washington attracted over 200,000 people of all races and backgrounds. They were there to protest racial discrimination. Their presence also showed support for important civil rights legislation in Congress. It was the largest political demonstration in the country's history at the time.

Many different leaders spoke that afternoon. Martin Luther King Jr. spoke at the end of the day. He delivered what many think of as his most memorable speech. He proclaimed, "I have a dream that one day this nation will rise up and live out the true meaning of its creed: 'We hold these truths to be self-evident: that all men are created equal.'"

A step toward that equality was taken with the passage of the Civil Rights Act in 1964. This act ended legal discrimination, but unfair practices continued. Throughout the South, African Americans were kept from or discouraged from voting. Local officials often did things to make people afraid to vote. They even did things so people couldn't register to vote. Groups that protested these "scare" tactics were met with violence. To protest these tactics, several leaders worked together to plan a peaceful march that would start in Selma, Alabama. It would end 50 miles away in the capital, Montgomery. There, the leaders hoped to present a petition to the governor that described the problems with voting and with their treatment by police.

The governor responded by making the march illegal. Even so, about 600 people gathered on Sunday, March 7, 1965. John Lewis, a well-known activist, was at the very front of the protest when they began to cross a bridge that led out of Selma. At the other end, Sheriff Clark and local and state police stopped them. Many police officers were on horseback and carried weapons, as well as gas masks to protect themselves against tear gas. They ordered the long line of marchers to turn around and return to the church where they had started.

The marchers refused, and someone gave the order to attack. Many photographers and TV crews recorded what happened. People all over the country saw pictures and TV clips of the Alabama police officers attacking the unarmed marchers. This included many women and children. More than a dozen demonstrators ended up in the hospital. The sight of this brutal behavior caused a strong reaction. Some people came to Selma in support. Thousands of others demonstrated in other cities to make their feelings known.

In response, President Lyndon B. Johnson presented legislation that became the Voting Rights Act of 1965. This act abolished literacy tests as a requirement for voting. It also allowed for federal supervision of certain districts suspected of unfair restrictions in the past.

With this act, many of the political goals of the civil rights movement had been achieved. The efforts of the courageous protesters made Dr. King's dream more of a reality.

Source #3

You have found an article that discusses *Brown v. Board of Education*, an important legal case that helped end segregation.

Civil Rights and the Supreme Court

In John Lewis and Rosa Parks's time, blacks and whites were segregated, or separated, in the South. They had separate drinking fountains, separate restaurants, and separate seats on public transportation. There was even segregation in schools. White children went to one school. Black children went to a different school. The schools the black children went to were not as good as the ones the white children went to. While the Fourteenth Amendment of the Constitution of the United States established that "no State . . . shall deny to any person equal protection of the law," African Americans had to deal with worse conditions in many areas.

A case brought before the Supreme Court of the United States in 1864, *Plessy v. Ferguson*, challenged this practice. The Supreme Court ruled that segregation was not a violation of the Constitution in that case. It said that as long as blacks received equal treatment, it was acceptable to separate them from whites. This meant that there could be separate schools for black students and white students as long as the quality of education was equal.

The problem was that blacks, including black children, did *not* receive equal treatment in any way. Segregated schools were visibly not equal to white schools in terms of buildings, educational materials, offerings, and teacher experience. In many southern states, black students who graduated from high school were not allowed to attend colleges for whites.

In Topeka, Kansas, in 1954, Oliver Brown and a number of other parties became plaintiffs against the state's board of education. A plaintiff is a person who sues another person or an organization. Brown and his co-plaintiffs were encouraged to do this by the National Association for the Advancement of Colored People (NAACP). Oliver Brown was a welder for a railroad company and had a daughter named Linda. They lived in an integrated neighborhood, but she had to go to a black school. Brown wanted his daughter to be able to attend the local white school. He enrolled her, but the board did not let her in because she was black.

In 1951, 13 families had brought a similar case against the board after they had tried to enroll their children in neighborhood schools that served white children. They lost that case. Brown, however, would take his case all the way to the Supreme Court.

Brown's attorney was Thurgood Marshall. He was chief attorney for the NAACP. The court case was not an easy battle. While seven justices agreed, two disagreed. Justice Earl Warren then took on the cause. He tried to get the others to agree with him. In a moving speech, Warren convinced the two dissenting justices that the only reason for a pro-segregation decision was a natural belief that blacks were inferior to whites. Justice Warren also argued that overturning the earlier case of *Plessy v. Ferguson* was the only way to maintain the integrity of the court. The case was decided with all justices voting for Brown. The case found that "separate educational facilities are inherently inequal."

Many schools in the South made an attempt at integration, but schools in the Deep South did all that they could to avoid it completely. One of the most dramatic examples of resisting integration happened in Little Rock, Arkansas, in 1957. Nine black students had been chosen to attend Little Rock's Central High School. Their selection was based on their overall academic excellence. When the students tried to enter the school, they were met with major resistance. Orval Faubus, governor of Arkansas, even called out the National Guard to prevent the students from entering. President Dwight D. Eisenhower had to get involved. He sent federal troops to take over. Eventually, the nine were escorted into the school under armed guard.

Name _____ Date _____

1 What were some of the major events that contributed to the rise of civil rights? Give details from at least **two** sources to support your answer.

_____

_____

_____

_____

_____

2 What are examples of specific responses to the civil rights movement? From these reactions, what conclusion can you draw about the initial support the movement received? Give details from at least **two** sources to support your answer.

_____

_____

_____

_____

_____

_____

3 Mark the boxes to match each source with the author's purpose that it supports. Some purposes may have more than one source selected.

	Source #1: John Lewis	Source #2: Civil Rights for All	Source #3: Civil Rights and the Supreme Court
To teach about the civil rights movement			
To give information about several events that signaled a rise in the civil rights movement			
To describe a legal case that helped put an end to "separate but equal" in the education system			
To give information on a single person's impact on the civil rights movement			

Part 2

You will now review your notes and sources, and plan, draft, revise, and edit your writing. You may use your notes and go back to the sources. Now read your assignment and the information about how your writing will be scored; then begin your work.

Your Assignment:

Your teacher wants each student to write an informational article that will explain a particular era in the twentieth century. Your article will be read by other students, teachers, and parents.

Using more than one source, develop a main idea about civil rights and how they evolved. Choose the most important information from more than one source to support your main idea. Then, write an informational article about your main idea that is several paragraphs long. Clearly organize your article and support your main idea with details from the sources. Use your own words except when quoting directly from the sources. Be sure to give the source title or number when using details from the sources.

REMEMBER: A well-written informational article

- has a clear main idea.
- is well-organized and stays on the topic.
- has an introduction and conclusion.
- uses transitions.
- uses details from the sources to support your main idea.
- puts the information from the sources in your own words, except when using direct quotations from the sources.
- gives the title or number of the source for the details or facts you included.
- develops ideas clearly.
- uses clear language.
- follows rules of writing (spelling, punctuation, and grammar usage).

Now begin work on your informational article. Manage your time carefully so that you can

1. plan your informational article.
2. write your informational article.
3. revise and edit the final draft of your informational article.

88

Name _____ Date _____

For Part 2, you are being asked to write an informational article that is several paragraphs long. Write your response in the space below.

Remember to check your notes and your prewriting and planning as you write, and then revise and edit your informational article.

_____

_____

_____

_____

_____

_____

_____

_____

_____

_____

_____

_____

_____

_____

_____

_____

_____

_____

_____

_____

_____

_____

Name _____ Date _____

Name _____ Date _____

_____

_____

_____

_____

_____

_____

_____

_____

_____

_____

_____

_____

_____

_____

_____

_____

_____

_____

_____

_____

_____

_____

Assessment 3
Reading

Read the text. Then answer the questions.

Help for the Homeless

"No one should have to eat out of a garbage can." That's the vision that Hannah Taylor had when she started her Ladybug Foundation to raise money to help the homeless.

When Hannah was just five years old, she saw a homeless man looking for something to eat around a garbage bin. Soon after, she observed a woman walking down the street, pushing everything she owned in a shopping cart in front of her. The contrast between Hannah's life and the lives of those she saw living on the street disturbed her. She had a warm, safe home in Canada, and she felt everybody deserved the same. Hannah worked with her mother to think of a way that she could help change the situation.

She discovered that families with children make up the fastest-growing group of people without homes. Because the cost of housing has risen without a rise in wages, many people are unable to afford housing. As a result, the number of people without homes has increased.

Armed with her new understanding, Hannah launched her action plan. She asked her teacher if she could speak to her classmates, and when her teacher said yes, she shared what she had learned with the other students. Together, she and her classmates decided to hold a bake sale and give the proceeds to a homeless shelter.

That was just the beginning for Hannah, however. Hannah decided that if she told people about homelessness, they would want to help, so she set out to spread the word. She adopted the ladybug as an emblem because it represents good luck. For Canada's "Make Change" month, Hannah and her mom spray-painted hundreds of baby food jars bright red. Then, Hannah pasted on black dots. When she thought the jars looked something like ladybugs, she put them in stores and schools to collect spare change, believing that even a minimum donation could help. "Make Change" month calls for people to give any of their spare change to a good cause. Hannah's ladybug jars can still be found throughout Canada today, helping to raise money for the homeless.

Hannah then broadened her target audience. At first, Hannah began taking local business leaders to lunch to ask for their help. Then, Hannah came up with an even bigger idea. With the help of her parents and business friends, Hannah organized her first Big Boss lunch. She believed that people in the business community—the "Big Bosses," as she called them—might become effective advocates for raising both awareness and funds for homeless programs if she could just speak to them about how they could help. This Big Boss lunch helped Hannah reach a large number of people in just one afternoon.

In 2004, Hannah and her supporters started the Ladybug Foundation. Foundations use their money to support important causes. Since its inception, the Ladybug Foundation has raised more than two million dollars to sustain homeless projects in Canada. The foundation helps fund many organizations that work with the homeless population in various ways. Many of the organizations that benefit share Hannah's belief that the homeless should be given immediate aid. Over 50 soup kitchens, emergency shelters, missions, youth shelters, and food banks have received financial help from her foundation.

Hannah's original vision has grown. Her Big Boss lunches continue and have resulted in foundation support from some of the largest companies in Canada. She travels widely, talking to groups about homelessness. She has also started a second foundation to educate people about charity.

A multimedia resource, makeChange: The Ladybug Foundation Education Program is designed to be used in schools. Its purpose is to inspire students to find their own cause in their community and bring about change through their own actions. Through her Ladybug Foundation, Hannah has learned the importance of giving back and how rewarding it is to help. She now wants to share this knowledge with other students and help them realize their own vision to make a difference. The makeChange program does just that.

Hannah's work has gained her recognition. In 2007, when she was eleven years old, Hannah won a Brick Award, which recognizes young people who are making a positive contribution to their communities. Perhaps most of all, Hannah values the friends she has made among the homeless. "They all have an individual story," she says.

Name _____ Date _____

1 Read the sentence from the text.

Since its <u>inception</u>, the Ladybug Foundation has raised more than two million dollars to sustain homeless projects in Canada.

What is the meaning of the word <u>inception</u> as it is used in the text?

Ⓐ beginning

Ⓑ assistance

Ⓒ company

Ⓓ interest

2 Which events led Hannah and her classmates to hold a bake sale to help the homeless? Select **three** options.

Ⓐ Soon after, she observed a woman walking down the street, pushing everything she owned in a shopping cart in front of her.

Ⓑ She discovered that families with children make up the fastest-growing group of people without homes.

Ⓒ She asked her teacher if she could speak to her classmates, and when her teacher said yes, she shared what she had learned with the other students.

Ⓓ She adopted the ladybug as an emblem because it represents good luck.

Ⓔ With the help of her parents and business friends, Hannah organized her first Big Boss lunch.

3 Which details from the text illustrate the idea that the Ladybug Foundation supports the homeless in Canada? Select **two** options.

   Ⓐ   She has also started a second foundation to educate people about charity.

   Ⓑ   Perhaps most of all, Hannah values the friends she has made among the homeless.

   Ⓒ   The foundation helps fund many organizations that work with the homeless population in various ways.

   Ⓓ   Over 50 soup kitchens, emergency shelters, missions, youth shelters, and food banks have received financial help from her foundation.

   Ⓔ   She believed that people in the business community—the "Big Bosses," as she called them—might become effective advocates for raising both awareness and funds for homeless programs if she could just speak to them about how they could help.

4 Read the following paragraphs from the text.

> When Hannah was just five years old, she saw a homeless man looking for something to eat around a garbage bin. Soon after, she observed a woman walking down the street, pushing everything she owned in a shopping cart in front of her. The contrast between Hannah's life and the lives of those she saw living on the street disturbed her. She had a warm, safe home in Canada, and she felt everybody deserved the same. Hannah worked with her mother to think of a way that she could help change the situation.
>
> She discovered that families with children make up the fastest-growing group of people without homes. Because the cost of housing has risen without a rise in wages, many people are unable to afford housing. As a result, the number of people without homes has increased.

Underline the **three** details in the text that **best** support the conclusion that Hannah cares about her community.

Name _____ Date _____

Read the text. Then answer the questions.

A Baseball League for Women

World War II affected every aspect of American life, including baseball. Many major-league ballplayers signed up for the military, so teams had trouble finding enough qualified players to fill their rosters. In order to field a full team, owners brought up players from minor-league teams. Unfortunately, this left minor-league teams with so few men that they had to stop playing altogether. In addition to the problems facing minor-league baseball, there was also a fear that major-league ballparks would share the same fate.

Chicago Cubs owner Philip K. Wrigley wondered what would bring crowds back to the empty minor-league stadiums and shore up major-league baseball as well. Wrigley asked one of his employees to form and head a committee to explore possible solutions to the baseball problem. After much discussion, the committee announced its idea: professional women's softball played on the minor-league fields. This idea was not without controversy. In the 1940s, women playing sports was considered unladylike; nevertheless, in 1943, Wrigley and his friends set up what was eventually named the All-American Girls Professional Baseball League.

Wrigley's group decided that the women's teams would play in minor-league stadiums throughout the Midwest. The league had four teams in its first year: the Kenosha Comets and the Racine Belles in Wisconsin, the Rockford Peaches in Illinois, and the South Bend Blue Sox in Indiana. The players came from amateur women's softball leagues in the United States and Canada. More than one hundred women were invited to attend spring training in 1943 at Wrigley Field in Chicago.

Each team had fifteen players, a manager, a business manager, and a female chaperone. The chaperone made sure players obeyed all the rules the league had set for them outside of the baseball stadium. In addition, players had to attend "charm school" to learn how to appear ladylike at all times. Many players didn't like these extra rules; however, they were thrilled to be away from home and to be paid to play the sport they loved.

The first season lasted from late May through September in 1943, with each team playing 108 games. Before the season began, some sportswriters wrote skeptical articles about the league's chance for success. They thought the female players would embarrass themselves because they could not play the game well enough.

Name _____ Date _____

They were very wrong. The season was a great success! More than 175,000 fans turned out to watch the games, and they were delighted by the quality and the enthusiasm of play. Ideas were changing in the United States, due in large part to the war effort. Women were entering the workforce in record numbers to fill jobs left by men who had joined the armed services. Americans were ready to accept women playing professional sports. One of the most popular players was Dottie Schroeder, a slick-fielding shortstop admired for her quickness and grace on the field, and her rocket-powered throwing arm.

In the first year of play, the league founders decided that the women would play by softball rules. The men did not think women could play hardball and pitch overhand. After the first few seasons, though, when the players' talent became clear, the league switched to regular baseball rules.

World War II ended in 1945, and many male baseball players returned to their teams. But by that point, the league had carved out its own place in the sports world. Two more women's teams were added in 1944, two in 1946, and two more after that in 1948. The post-war success was short-lived, however. After a high point in 1948, when more than 900,000 fans attended games, the league rapidly lost popularity. The All-American Girls Professional Baseball League played its last season in 1954.

What caused this sudden loss of interest on the part of the fans? The answer was television. The early 1950s marked the beginning of the television age; in each year of that decade, millions of people bought their first television set. Sports, especially baseball, were popular on the new medium. Families that used to go out to watch sports now stayed at home to watch them. The All-American Girls Professional Baseball League became a victim of progress; nonetheless, professional women's baseball had had its moment in the sun, and it had shone brightly.

---

5 Read the sentence from the text.

> Before the season began, some sportswriters wrote
> skeptical articles about the league's chance for success.

Which word means the same as skeptical but has a more negative connotation?

- Ⓐ doubtful
- Ⓑ suspicious
- Ⓒ questioning
- Ⓓ unconvinced

Name _____ Date _____

6 What was **most likely** the author's purpose for writing this text?

Ⓐ to give information about the history of the All-American Girls Professional Baseball League

Ⓑ to entertain readers with stories of players in the All-American Girls Professional Baseball League

Ⓒ to persuade readers that the All-American Girls Professional Baseball League should be brought back

Ⓓ to explain how the game of baseball was played in the All-American Girls Professional Baseball League

7 Read the sentence from the text.

But by that point, <u>the league had carved out its own place</u> in the sports world.

What is the meaning of <u>the league had carved out its own place</u> as it is used in the text?

Ⓐ The league made its own spot in the realm of sports.

Ⓑ The league forced the men's minor-league teams to close.

Ⓒ The league beat other leagues in games to create its own place.

Ⓓ The league became unpopular among fans of professional sports.

8 Which details illustrate why Dottie Schroeder was popular? Select **two** options.

Ⓐ Dottie was a shortstop.

Ⓑ Dottie was quick and graceful on the field.

Ⓒ Dottie had a rocket-powered throwing arm.

Ⓓ Dottie was one of the most popular players on the team.

Ⓔ Dottie was a player in the All-American Girls Professional Baseball League.

Read the text. Then answer the questions.

A Bold Challenge

On April 12, 1961, Yuri Gagarin, a cosmonaut from the former Soviet Union, orbited Earth in a space capsule called *Vostok 1*. He was nearly 200 miles above Earth. The capsule traveled at 18,000 miles per hour. The orbit took a total of 108 minutes. The 27-year-old test pilot parachuted back to Earth, with the distinction of being the first human to travel into space. He reported that he felt fine after the trip, and he put to rest any fears that humans could not survive such a voyage.

About a month later, on May 25, 1961, in response to the Soviets' accomplishment, President John F. Kennedy stood before Congress. He was about to make one of the most important speeches of his presidency. At the time, the United States and the Soviet Union were caught up in the Cold War. In this war, the two enemies did not fight directly. Instead, they tried to gain power by forging ties with other nations and outdoing one another in scientific research. Still, the possibility of war always loomed. Each superpower had enough nuclear weapons to destroy the other. And now, the Soviet Union had taken the lead in a vital area—the race to explore space.

President Kennedy understood that the United States needed to respond. The Soviets had shown the world that they had better technology. This might help them win new ties with other nations and possibly weaken the United States' standing in the world. Perhaps more importantly, the powerful rockets the Soviets had used to carry a human into space could also be used to launch nuclear weapons. If the Soviets gained too much of an advantage in rocket science, it might increase the likelihood of an attack on the United States. The Soviet Union might have the upper hand.

Not only in Congress, but also across America, people awaited the president's response. Most had no idea how bold it would be. The president and his advisers knew it was highly likely that the Soviets would build on Gagarin's success. They would probably soon have the ability to send a multi-passenger spacecraft in a path around Earth. The next step would be to orbit the moon. In a shrewd move, the president decided to focus on landing on the moon by 1970. Accomplishing this would require both countries to develop different rockets and new technology, giving the Americans an even chance to compete. In addition, landing on the moon would be an amazing, morale-boosting achievement for the United States.

In his address, President Kennedy asked Congress to provide billions of dollars to reach this goal. He explained why it was so important to land on the moon and why so much money would be needed to accomplish this feat:

> No single space project in this period will be more impressive to mankind, or more important to the long-range exploration of space; and none will be so difficult or expensive to accomplish. We propose to accelerate the development of the appropriate lunar spacecraft. We propose to develop alternate liquid and solid fuel boosters, much larger than any now being developed, until certain which is superior. We propose additional funds for other engine development and for unmanned explorations—explorations which are particularly important for one purpose which this nation will never overlook: the survival of the man who first makes this daring flight. But in a very real sense, it will not be one man going to the moon—if we make this judgment affirmatively, it will be an entire nation. For all of us must work to put him there.

The youngest president voted into office in American history, John F. Kennedy showed his vision by setting this bold challenge before the country. At the time, only one suborbital flight had been executed by the United States. However, the mission was accomplished. On July 20, 1969, *Apollo 11* astronauts Buzz Aldrin and Neil Armstrong walked on the moon's surface. To the Americans watching, Armstrong sent this memorable message: "That's one small step for (a) man, one giant leap for mankind."

Sadly, before he could witness the success of the moon landing, President Kennedy was assassinated. However, for the people of the United States, his dream of space as the "New Frontier" lives on.

Name _____ Date _____

9 Read the sentence from the text.

"We propose additional funds for other engine development and for <u>unmanned</u> explorations—explorations which are particularly important for one purpose which this nation will never overlook: the survival of the man who first makes this daring flight."

What does the word <u>unmanned</u> mean as it is used in the sentence?

Ⓐ not carrying a person

Ⓑ back to carrying a person

Ⓒ before carrying a person

Ⓓ against carrying a person

10 This question has two parts. First, answer part A. Then, answer part B.

Part A

Which statement **best** describes the central idea of this text?

Ⓐ President Kennedy decided to focus on landing on the moon.

Ⓑ Buzz Aldrin and Neil Armstrong landed on the moon on July 20, 1969.

Ⓒ President Kennedy asked all Americans to work to put a man on the moon.

Ⓓ Landing on the moon was a result of the Cold War between America and the Soviet Union.

Part B

Which detail from the text **best** supports the answer to part A?

Ⓐ In addition, landing on the moon would be an amazing, morale-boosting achievement for the United States.

Ⓑ If the Soviets gained too much of an advantage in rocket science, it might increase the likelihood of an attack on the United States.

Ⓒ To the Americans watching, Armstrong sent this memorable message: "That's one small step for (a) man, one giant leap for mankind."

Ⓓ "But in a very real sense, it will not be one man going to the moon—if we make this judgment affirmatively, it will be an entire nation."

11 Read the sentence from the text.

In a shrewd move, the president decided to focus on landing on the moon by 1970.

Is this claim from the text supported by reasons and evidence? Why or why not? Use details from the text to support your response.

_____

_____

_____

_____

 12 Read the sentences from the text.

The Soviets had shown the world that they had better technology. This might help them win new ties with other nations and possibly weaken the United States' standing in the world. Perhaps more importantly, the powerful rockets the Soviets had used to carry a human into space could also be used to launch nuclear weapons. If the Soviets gained too much of an advantage in rocket science, it might increase the likelihood of an attack on the United States.

How do these sentences develop the idea that Kennedy's speech to Congress about the Soviets' accomplishment was one of the most important speeches of his presidency?

Ⓐ They explain why the Soviets' accomplishment was a threat to America.

Ⓑ They explain how America's accomplishments would lead to the Cold War.

Ⓒ They explain how the Soviets' accomplishment erased the fear of traveling in space.

Ⓓ They explain why President Kennedy chose landing on the moon as America's next accomplishment.

Name _____ Date _____

Read the text. Then answer the questions.

Louis Steps Up

Thanksgiving Day dawned cloudy and cold. On Friday, the snow began to fall, at first in big flakes floating gently downward to frost the ground, and later gathering momentum to heap one on top of the other. On Saturday, the wind drove sheets of ice over everything. The storm was now officially termed a blizzard. By Sunday, sections of the city were without power, and roads were not passable.

In his dormitory, Louis and the six other boarding-school students who had stayed on campus for the holiday weekend huddled closer to the fire roaring in the massive fireplace. "Can you see your breath yet?" Louis joked, and the other boys grinned.

"Who knows when the city will be back to normal?" said Demetri.

Just then, Louis's cell phone lit up and blared a loud ringtone. Luckily, there was still some battery power left in the thing. "Hey," he answered, and then, after a momentary pause, said, "Hi, Mark. What's up?" Louis's voice expressed his surprise at hearing from Mark Brovar, an eighth grader at the school and the editor of the *Granville Middle School Newspaper*. Louis listened intently as the voice on the other end spoke to him. He could feel the other students' eyes on him. "Hmm. Okay. The regular phones are still working, but we don't have power." There was another pause, and then Louis said, "All right. Yes. I should be able to use the slower dial-up Internet connection. I can't guarantee anything, but I will give it my best shot. Talk to you later."

"What did Mark want?" queried Demetri curiously when Louis ended the call.

"Well, Mark is responsible for the front-page article for the next edition of the newspaper. The draft is on his desktop computer, and he really needs to revise it before Tuesday's deadline. The airport is still closed, so he doesn't know if he will even be back by Tuesday. He asked me to email the article to him so that he can use his laptop to work on it. When I told him that we have no power and I can't turn on his desktop computer, he asked that I do him a huge favor. There is a hard copy of the first draft on his desk, and he wondered if I would type it into my laptop and send it to him. I think it still has enough juice."

"That sounds like a plan," said Demetri. "Why did you sound so tentative on the phone?"

Name _____ Date _____

"Well, Mark didn't have his laptop with him when he interviewed Mr. Hadley. Since he is blind, he had to take his notes and write his first draft in Braille. Before I can get to work, I need a crash course in Braille! Listen, I'll see you guys later. I had better get going!"

"Good luck," they called as Louis hurried out of the warm lounge.

Fortunately, Louis already had a slight familiarity with Braille. He knew that it involved using a pen-like instrument called a stylus to make a pattern of holes representing letters of the alphabet. After seeing Mark write a note to his parents, Louis had become eager to find out more about the language. He had taken out a book from the library with a chart identifying what letter each pattern stood for. He still had that book on his own desk.

After finding the article draft on Mark's desk in the newspaper office, Louis returned to his dorm room, threw on an extra blanket and a pair of socks, and began to work. He had always been fascinated by secret codes and felt like a master spy as he transcribed what Mark had written, carefully running his fingertips over the patterns to make sure he had each letter right. Two hours later, he looked up, astonished at how much time had elapsed. His laptop battery was running low, so he had to be quick, since the power was still out. After reviewing the text on his screen, he quickly connected to the Internet with the phone cable and emailed the article to Mark.

Surprisingly, the power came on a few hours later, and the returning students began to straggle in the next day as roads and airports reopened. Mark returned to school on Tuesday, and as soon as he dropped off his things in his room, he immediately sought out Louis. "Louis," said the grateful editor, clapping him on the shoulder, "you have no idea how much stress you saved me. What you did went above and beyond the duty of a staff member. We don't usually give big assignments to sixth graders, but for the next issue, I would like you to work with me on the lead story."

13 Read the sentence from the text.

> By Sunday, sections of the city were without power, and roads were not <u>passable</u>.

What is the meaning of the word <u>passable</u> as it is used in the sentence?

Ⓐ passing before

Ⓑ can pass over

Ⓒ difficult to pass

Ⓓ done in a passing way

14 Read the paragraph from the text.

> "Well, Mark is responsible for the front-page article for the next edition of the newspaper. The draft is on his desktop computer, and he really needs to revise it before Tuesday's deadline. The airport is still closed, so he doesn't know if he will even be back by Tuesday. He asked me to email the article to him so that he can use his laptop to work on it. When I told him that we have no power and I can't turn on his desktop computer, he asked that I do him a huge favor. There is a hard copy of the first draft on his desk, and he wondered if I would type it into my laptop and send it to him. I think it still has enough juice."

Underline the sentence that illustrates how the setting affects the plot of the text.

Name _____   Date _____

15   This question has two parts. First, answer part A. Then, answer part B.

Part A

   How is Louis different at the end of the story?

   Ⓐ   He has learned to read Braille.

   Ⓑ   He has researched languages.

   Ⓒ   He has become the editor of the newspaper.

   Ⓓ   He has learned how to use a dial-up Internet connection.

Part B

   Which detail from the text **best** supports the answer to part A?

   Ⓐ   He had taken out a book from the library with a chart identifying what letter each pattern stood for.

   Ⓑ   He had always been fascinated by secret codes and felt like a master spy as he transcribed what Mark had written, carefully running his fingertips over the patterns to make sure he had each letter right.

   Ⓒ   After reviewing the text on his screen, he quickly connected to the Internet with the phone cable and emailed the article to Mark.

   Ⓓ   "We don't usually give big assignments to sixth graders, but for the next issue, I would like you to work with me on the lead story."

16   Read the sentences from the text.

   "That sounds like a plan," said Demetri. "Why did you sound so <u>tentative</u> on the phone?"

What does the word <u>tentative</u> help the reader understand about Louis?

   Ⓐ   He is unable to help Mark.

   Ⓑ   He is excited about helping Mark.

   Ⓒ   He is hesitant about helping Mark.

   Ⓓ   He is confident that he can help Mark.

Read the text. Then answer the questions.

Felicia's Audition

Felicia bowed to the audience, an elegant figure in black velvet, lightly grasping the neck of her cello as the delirious crowd chanted, "Brava, brava, brava!" With a dignified wave and a brilliant smile, Felicia the World-Renowned Cellist left the stage.

"Felicia," her mother called, "Finish up your homework, because dinner is ready and just about to be on the table!" Felicia jumped, startled by the sound of her mother's voice disturbing the middle of her daydream. Guiltily, she returned to reality, refocused on her math homework, solved the last equation, and packed up her books. Now reminded of school, Felicia sighed. She wouldn't say that she despised it, but she certainly did not embrace it with joy or interest. Because she had not yet formed a single friendship since her family had moved here, this transition to her new school was proving to be especially difficult to navigate.

On Friday morning, Felicia was struggling through the crowds in the hallway to get to her locker when she overheard a group of students talking animatedly. "An orchestra? I can't believe there are enough talented people in this school to form one!" exclaimed one girl in surprise.

"Since so many schools in the area have orchestras, after careful consideration, our school board thought we should, too," said the other knowingly.

"Do you think you will audition?" one girl asked as they moved past Felicia, not noticing her staring after them and straining to hear their conversation. The voices faded as the group sauntered down the hall, becoming fainter as they turned the corner, and finally disappearing entirely. Felicia felt her heart accelerate at the thought of belonging to an actual orchestra. It would be an actual dream come true. And maybe she could meet some other students as a bonus.

At the end of the day, the rumor was confirmed, and Felicia could barely contain her excitement. "Auditions for the school orchestra are scheduled for next Thursday," announced the principal over the loudspeaker, "and players of all instruments are encouraged to attend." Visions of her and her cello residing in first chair danced across her mind.

Felicia hurried home, feeling more exuberant than she had since the move. "Mom, I cannot be disturbed this weekend. I have to practice for my orchestra audition. Don't ask me to cook or clean or even take part in family game night! I must devote myself to my art. This audition could make my school career!" she proclaimed dramatically.

By Thursday, in spite of all her practicing, Felicia was sick with nervousness. She had never wanted anything more fervently than to belong in the orchestra. To compose herself and get in a final practice, she crept into an empty classroom to run through her music selection for the last time. Halfway through the impromptu rehearsal, the A string snapped without warning. Felicia gasped as she realized that she had made no provisions for this possibility. Crushed and believing her chance of a lifetime was destroyed before it had even begun, she packed up her instrument and her bow, and trudged back to the audition room with tears streaming down her face, prepared to explain why she wouldn't be auditioning after all. A girl hovering outside the door approached her tentatively when she saw how upset Felicia looked. "Hey, Felicia, I am Amara Goodman. I'm in your homeroom. You seem upset. Is something wrong? Maybe I can help."

Sobbing, Felicia explained what had happened. "My dream is to someday become a famous cellist," she said, hiccupping. "But I really want to be in the school orchestra because then maybe I would at least feel a part of this school," she finished with a gulp.

"Wait here a second," said Amara. "I'll be right back." She disappeared into the audition room and came out a minute later followed by a kind-looking man.

"Hi, Felicia," he said, smiling down at her. "I am Mr. Goodman, orchestra director and Amara's father. I hear you just suffered a cello catastrophe. Well, we really need cellists in this orchestra, and I happen to have a school instrument available. Do you want to give it a whirl with that?"

A vision of Felicia the World-Renowned Cellist glided through her mind. She couldn't give up on this challenge when she was so close to her desired achievement. "Yes," she said with determination. At the end of her audition, not even the standing ovation of the imaginary crowds could have meant more to Felicia than the enthusiastic applause of Amara and her dad.

"You're in!" said Mr. Goodman.

"You were brilliant!" exclaimed Amara. "And guess what? I am in the orchestra, too, so I think we'll be seeing a lot of each other, starting tomorrow in homeroom. I'll change seats so that I can sit next to you! We're going to have a lot of fun this year!"

Happily, Felicia agreed.

17 Read the sentence from the text.

"This audition could make my school career!" she proclaimed dramatically.

What does the word proclaimed mean as it is used in the text?

- Ⓐ to claim again
- Ⓑ to claim before
- Ⓒ to claim foolishly
- Ⓓ to claim confidently

18 This question has two parts. First, answer part A. Then, answer part B.

Part A

How does Felicia's point of view change at the end of the text?

- Ⓐ She believes she will like school.
- Ⓑ She is uninterested in making friends.
- Ⓒ She wants to be part of the orchestra.
- Ⓓ She thinks she will have a hard time fitting in.

Part B

Which detail from the text **best** supports the answer to part A?

- Ⓐ She wouldn't say that she despised it, but she certainly did not embrace it with joy or interest.
- Ⓑ "Mom, I cannot be disturbed this weekend. I have to practice for my orchestra audition."
- Ⓒ "My dream is to someday become a famous cellist," she said, hiccupping. "But I really want to be in the school orchestra, because then maybe I would at least feel a part of this school," she finished with a gulp.
- Ⓓ "We're going to have a lot of fun this year!" Happily, Felicia agreed.

Name _____ Date _____

19 Read the following sentence from the text.

> Felicia bowed to the audience, an <u>elegant</u> figure in black velvet, lightly grasping the neck of her cello as the delirious crowd chanted, "Brava, brava, brava!"

Which word means the opposite of <u>elegant</u> as used in the text?

   Ⓐ grateful

   Ⓑ plain

   Ⓒ nervous

   Ⓓ stylish

20 Does the school orchestra become important to Felicia? Why or why not? Include details from the text to support your answer.

_____

_____

_____

_____

_____

21 Read the sentence from the text.

> Crushed and believing her chance of a lifetime was destroyed before it had even begun, she packed up her instrument and her bow, and <u>trudged</u> back to the audition room with tears streaming down her face, prepared to explain why she wouldn't be auditioning after all.

What tone does the word <u>trudged</u> create in the text?

   Ⓐ upset

   Ⓑ longing

   Ⓒ reflective

   Ⓓ exhausted

Name _____   Date _____

Writing

Read and answer each question.

22   Paul is writing a story for class. He wants to revise to eliminate any misspelled words. Read a paragraph from his story, and complete the task that follows.

> When Juanita approached the airport gate, the airline attendant told her boarding had ended five minutes ago. Juanita was desperate to get on the flight, but even though it was visable through the airport window, the attendant stated the plane was inaccessible. The gate doors had officially closed. The attendant assured her she could get on another flight, but Juanita felt hopeless. What was supposed to be an enjoyible vacation was turning into a horrible nightmare.

Underline the **two** words that have spelling errors.

23   Choose the sentence that contains a spelling error.

    Ⓐ   Nora helped Eliot design the magazine cover.

    Ⓑ   Jimmy swept the crumbs off the kitchen floor.

    Ⓒ   Elizabeth daydreamed about a vacation on a warm iland.

    Ⓓ   The two shook hands before they began to wrestle.

24 Greg is writing a story about a hiking trip. He wants to revise to eliminate any errors. Read a paragraph from his story, and complete the task that follows.

> Evelyn nervously peered down the unfamiliar path, unsure which way to go next. <u>Her companion who was named Jessica searched the map for clues but couldn't locate their position.</u> When Evelyn remembered she brought a compass along, the weight seemed to lift off her shoulders, and she let out a huge sigh of relief. They would get home before sundown after all.

What revision **best** fixes the underlined sentence?

Ⓐ Her companion who was named Jessica, searched the map for clues but couldn't locate their position.

Ⓑ Her companion who was named, Jessica searched the map for clues but couldn't locate their position.

Ⓒ Her companion who was named (Jessica) searched the map for clues but couldn't locate their position.

Ⓓ Her companion, who was named Jessica, searched the map for clues but couldn't locate their position.

25 Monika wrote a research report about Glacier National Park. Read the paragraph and think about the changes she should make.

> Glacier National Park is located in the northern Rocky Mountains of Montana. My parents took my brother and me there one summer, and we thought it was so beautiful. Glacier National Park adjoins Canada's Waterton Lakes National Park. Flathead River and Flathead National Forest are west and southwest of Glacier National Park. Lewis and Clark National Forest and Blackfeet Indian Reservation are east and southeast of the park. There are several campgrounds in the park. My family loved sleeping under the stars at Fish Creek Campground.

Underline the **two** sentences that are not necessary to include in the paragraph.

Name _____ Date _____

26 Sapna is writing an opinion essay about the benefits of wearing school uniforms. Read the draft of her first paragraph, and complete the task that follows.

School uniforms are beneficial to students in several ways. First of all, school uniforms <u>make more</u> school spirit because they help build a sense of community within the school. Second, school uniforms keep students focused on learning instead of fashion. Last, school uniforms are cost-effective, because students don't have to buy other clothes for school.

The writer wants to replace the underlined phrase to make her meaning clearer. Which **three** words would be better choices?

Ⓐ boost

Ⓑ relieve

Ⓒ improve

Ⓓ increase

Ⓔ connect

Ⓕ complicate

27 Which of the following sentences has an error in comma usage?

Ⓐ Piper, my youngest sister, has always been a handful.

Ⓑ The latest thriller out in theaters *Run Faster* is a must see!

Ⓒ The students who hand in incomplete homework will receive a zero.

Ⓓ My father, an avid reader, recommends the book *Greetings from Mr. Edgarton*.

28 Which sentence includes an intensive pronoun?

Ⓐ Someone ate all of the cookies right off the pan.

Ⓑ This was a very selfish thing to do.

Ⓒ What should the consequences be for the thief?

Ⓓ I myself believe that the punishment should fit the crime.

Name _____ Date _____

29 A student is writing a report about Royal Albert Hall. The student needs to use words that are clear and specific in his report. Read the paragraph from the draft of the report and answer the question that follows.

> Royal Albert Hall is a concert hall located in Westminster, London. It was known for having <u>less than perfect</u> acoustics because of its echo. In the late 1960s, improvements were made and its echo <u>was fixed to a large degree</u>. Many different types of events take place at Royal Albert Hall, including concerts, sporting events, festivals, and balls.

Which set of words **best** replaces the underlined phrases with clearer and more-specific language?

Ⓐ poor, greatly decreased

Ⓑ imperfect, highly worsened

Ⓒ faulty, formed

Ⓓ wild, resolved

30 Jean-Claude is writing a paper about the importance of giving to charities. Read the draft of a paragraph from his paper, and answer the question that follows.

> If you are looking for a way to make a difference in your community, you should consider giving to charities. There are many reasons why giving to charities is important. Charities help people in need in a way that individuals alone cannot. Charities can <u>figure out</u> the people in need and determine how best to help them. Giving to charities also allows people to experience the wonderful feeling of connecting with others.

Jean-Claude wants to replace the underlined phrase to make his meaning more exact. Which word would make his word choice better?

Ⓐ emphasize

Ⓑ observe

Ⓒ master

Ⓓ identify

31 Mohammed is writing an informational paragraph for a class report about babysitting. The paragraph needs a conclusion to the topic. Read the paragraph and the directions that follow.

> Although babysitting can be a lot of fun, it is a responsibility that should not be taken lightly. The most important thing a babysitter must do is protect children from harm. Babysitters must constantly monitor children to ensure they are always safe. They must be sure the toys the children play with are suitable for their age. In addition, babysitters must have easy access to all important emergency phone numbers.

Write at least one sentence that could be added to the end of the paragraph to conclude the topic.

_____

_____

_____

_____

Listening

Listen to the presentation. Then answer the questions.

Life on the International Space Station

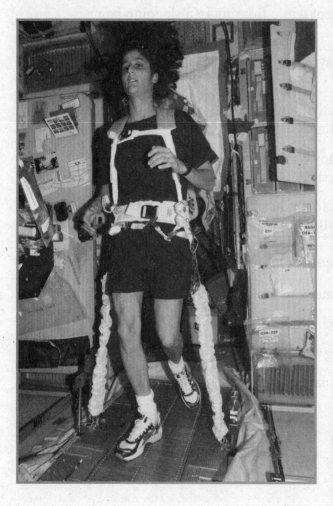

Name _____ Date _____

32 What is **most likely** the purpose of the presentation?

Ⓐ to describe a typical day on the space station

Ⓑ to give information about living on the space station

Ⓒ to persuade readers of the importance of the space station

Ⓓ to explain how astronauts adjust to lack of gravity in the space station

33 Which of the following details from the presentation support the idea that life on the space station is different than on Earth? Select **three** options.

Ⓐ Inside her cabin, Williams slept while floating in a sleeping bag attached to the wall.

Ⓑ Still, many astronauts can play games or read books to keep themselves busy.

Ⓒ "I didn't sit down for six months on the space station," commented astronaut Sunita "Suni" Williams.

Ⓓ They may be compact, but they contain quite a view—each cabin has a window for gazing out into space!

Ⓔ Williams kept books and photos of her family inside her cabin, which made it feel "like your own little house," she said.

34 Which conclusion is **best** supported by the information in the presentation?

Ⓐ There are no chairs on the International Space Station.

Ⓑ Astronauts on the International Space Station long to go home.

Ⓒ There are challenges to living on the International Space Station.

Ⓓ Astronauts on the International Space Station do not have any privacy.

118

Name _____ Date _____

Listen to the presentation. Then answer the questions.

What Can We Learn from Archaeology?

Name _____ Date _____

35 What is the main idea of the presentation?

Ⓐ Scientists use precise methods to discover artifacts.

Ⓑ Scientists want to recover artifacts without breaking them.

Ⓒ Scientists sort and analyze all of the artifacts they discover.

Ⓓ Scientists have different tools to find what might be under the ground.

36 This question has two parts. First, answer part A. Then, answer part B.

Part A

Which of the following is the **best** conclusion that can be drawn from the presentation?

Ⓐ Technology is helpful in archaeology.

Ⓑ Scientists study artifacts in laboratories.

Ⓒ Artifacts help us understand past civilizations.

Ⓓ Workers record the location where objects are found.

Part B

Which detail from the presentation **best** supports the answer to part A?

Ⓐ When workers discover an object, they catalog its exact location.

Ⓑ Excavated objects are carefully cleaned and studied in a laboratory to determine their age and what they are made of.

Ⓒ Through precise methods, archaeologists discover artifacts that reveal how people used to live, enabling us to understand much more about ancient cultures.

Ⓓ Sometimes they push long rods into the ground to get an idea of what might be underneath; however, GPS satellites make establishing an exact location much easier.

37 Which of the following **best** describes a key point in this presentation?

Ⓐ Archaeologists have learned little about ancient cultures.

Ⓑ Archaeologists work carefully so as to not destroy artifacts.

Ⓒ Archaeology is a new science that relies heavily on satellites.

Ⓓ Archaeology is the study of exploring new places by taking walks.

Name _____ Date _____

Listen to the presentation. Then answer the questions.

The Qin Dynasty

© Houghton Mifflin Harcourt Publishing Company. All rights reserved.

Name _____ Date _____

38 What is **most likely** the purpose of the presentation?

Ⓐ to explain how Qin Shi Huang ruled

Ⓑ to explain the effect of the Han dynasty

Ⓒ to give information about the Qin dynasty

Ⓓ to give information about legalist principles

39 Which of the following conclusions can be drawn from the presentation? Select **two** options.

Ⓐ Qin Shi Huang was not a kind ruler.

Ⓑ The Qin dynasty was not successful.

Ⓒ China has been ruled by only two dynasties.

Ⓓ The Qin dynasty lasted for 10,000 generations.

Ⓔ The people of China welcomed the imposition of legalist principles.

40 The passage includes key points about the Qin dynasty as well as some about the Han dynasty. Look at the points below and check the box to indicate the correct dynasty.

	Qin Dynasty	Han Dynasty
United China for the first time		
Ying Cheng was the first ruler.		
Liu Bang was the first ruler.		
Began in 202 BCE		

Research

Read and answer each question.

41 Miguel is reading scientific research and found these observations. Which **three** details support the conclusion that the new substance prevents cell growth in Dr. Greenberg's experiment?

Dr. Greenberg's observations about the new substance are as follows:

- When Cell A was combined with the new substance, no growth occurred.
- When Cell B was combined with the new substance and placed under heat, no growth occurred.
- When Cell C was placed under heat but was not combined with the substance, growth occurred.
- When twice the amount of the new substance was combined with Cell D, no growth occurred.

Ⓐ The new substance alone caused Cell C to grow.

Ⓑ The new substance alone did not cause Cell A to grow.

Ⓒ The new substance allowed Dr. Greenberg to observe cell growth.

Ⓓ The new substance combined with heat did not cause Cell B to grow.

Ⓔ The new substance caused growth when Cell A and Cell C were combined.

Ⓕ The new substance with twice the amount combined with Cell D did not cause growth.

42 A student is researching tsunamis and found this information. Read the paragraph and underline **three** effects that a tsunami can have once it reaches shore.

A tsunami is a long, high ocean wave. It is powerful enough to uproot trees. A tsunami occurs after a submarine earthquake, landslide, or volcano eruption takes place. These events create gigantic ocean waves that can be extremely destructive once they reach the coast. A tsunami is so forceful that it can destroy buildings and wash away entire beaches.

Name _____ Date _____

43 William is researching photography and came across this text.

An essential skill for any photographer shooting with film is creating a photograph from a negative. To do so, one must have a darkroom, which must be totally void of all light, in which to complete the following steps. First, use the negative to expose the image on photographic paper. Second, place the paper in a tray of developer, a chemical compound that converts the latent image, for 60 seconds. Next, move the paper to the stop bath and leave it there for 30 seconds. Then, place the paper in the fixer for at least 3 minutes. Finally, place the paper in the wash for 5 minutes.

What is the author's main purpose for writing the text?

Ⓐ   to teach

Ⓑ   to entertain

Ⓒ   to persuade

Ⓓ   to compare and contrast

44 A student is gathering research on Nelson Mandela and found this text. What conclusions can be made based on the details in the paragraph? Choose **three** answers.

Nelson Mandela was a black nationalist who lived from 1918 to 2013. Throughout his life, he fought against South Africa's apartheid system of racial segregation and spent 27 years in prison as a result. When he was released from prison, he remained focused and worked to finally put an end to apartheid. In 1993, he was awarded the prestigious Nobel Peace Prize. In 1994, he became the first black president of South Africa.

Ⓐ   Nelson Mandela was an exceptional leader.

Ⓑ   Nelson Mandela dedicated his life to his country.

Ⓒ   Prison allowed Mandela time to plan his future presidency.

Ⓓ   The Nobel Peace Prize is a very highly regarded award.

Ⓔ   Nelson Mandela ruled using forceful but effective measures.

Ⓕ   South Africa's system of apartheid was supported by the majority of South Africans.

Name _____ Date _____

45 Alyssa is doing research for an essay she is writing about lunch choices at school. She read the paragraph below. Underline the sentence that **best** illustrates that the author's purpose is to persuade.

> When I walked through the cafeteria at a local school, I saw students eating pizza and French fries. Others were sipping on calorie-filled sodas and juices. Good nutrition is important at school because many children eat at least half of their meals there. Even though it would come at a cost, it is very important that school lunches be improved to offer healthier options. This must include fruits, vegetables, and whole grains.

Name _____ Date _____

Performance Task 3
Part 1

Robot Technology

Task:

A group of students at your school is participating in a robotics competition. All the classes have decided to study robotics. Your class is studying the role that robots play in our lives. You decide to consider both the pros and cons of robots. You have found three sources about this topic in the school library.

After you have reviewed these sources, you will answer some questions about them. Briefly scan the sources and the three questions that follow. Then, go back and read the sources carefully so you will have the information you will need to answer the questions and complete your research. You may use scratch paper to take notes on the information you find in the sources as you read.

In Part 2, you will write an argumentative essay using information you have read.

Directions for Beginning:

You will now examine several sources. You can reexamine any of the sources as often as you like.

Research Questions:

After reviewing the sources, use the rest of the time in Part 1 to answer three questions about them. Your answers to these questions will be scored. Also, your answers will help you think about the information you have read, which should help you write your argumentative essay.

You may refer back to your scratch paper to review your notes when you think it would be helpful. Answer the questions in the spaces below the items.

Your written notes on scratch paper will be available to you in Part 1 and Part 2 of the performance task.

Name _____ Date _____

Source #1

You have found an article that describes the ways that human-like robots can benefit society.

Human Robots

In science fiction stories and films, humanoid robots—those with human characteristics—interact comfortably with people. Sometimes they even become a human's best friend! For many years, these high-tech robots have been only in the imaginations of writers and filmmakers. But with recent improvements in technology, they are becoming a reality.

Dr. Cynthia Breazeal is a pioneer in the research and development of "personal" robots at the Massachusetts Institute of Technology (MIT). Her interest was sparked by her exposure to the robots in the *Star Wars* movies. Awed by their "humanity," she made it her goal to build a robot that was socially intelligent.

Doing so involved thinking about how people communicate. There is the verbal, or language, part. Just as important, or even more so, is the nonverbal part. People convey meaning and signal emotions with their bodies through their gestures, posture, and movements. They display other nonverbal cues as well, such as their facial expressions or the direction of their gaze. When people interact, they make judgments about the credibility and likability of one another based on these nonverbal facets of their communication.

To facilitate a bond between a person and a robot, there had to be a level of nonverbal communication. The robot had to seem empathetic and trustworthy. Building in body language and nonverbal cues was the key to making a social relationship with a robot possible. Dr. Breazeal knew that people respond to these cues without realizing it, so it wouldn't matter if the cues came from a robot or from another person. The connection would still be there. The robots also had to respond to cues from the person. Being able to do this successfully would enable robots to learn. This, she hoped, would make them useful in a lot of situations.

Dr. Breazeal used this information to build the first social robot, Kismet, in the late 1990s. Kismet has eyes, eyebrows, a mouth, and ears. It can react with expressions to people. It moves its gaze, tilts its head, and changes its facial expression. Kismet also makes sounds in response to what a human is doing and saying.

Can this type of robot actually help people live better lives or achieve more? The answer is yes. While working at MIT, Dr. Cory Kidd developed Autom, a weight-loss coach robot. Autom has a simple molded plastic body that holds a touchscreen and a head that contains a camera and eyes. Autom has an artificial female voice. It is able to move its head so its eyes can follow the person with whom it is interacting.

The scientists at MIT were interested to see whether having information presented by a robot rather than a computer screen would be a better way to help people lose weight. They ran a trial in 2007 to find out. Some people in the trial kept a traditional diet log with pen and paper, while others were given a computer with the weight-loss program. The third group was given Autom. Autom's touchscreen had the same weight-loss program as the laptop. Those with Autom stayed on their diets the longest. As a result, they lost more weight and developed healthier habits. The feedback showed that these people viewed Autom as a more active coach. They wanted to do well on their diets because of Autom. Some even dressed their robot and were sad to lose it when the trial was over.

Social robots have moved out of the realm of fantasy and into the real world. Scientists like Dr. Breazeal do not see them as a replacement for humans. They see them as a way to make human existence better. For her, robots remain "all about people."

Source #2
You have found an article about the history of robots.

The First Robots

Imagine lying in a hospital bed and having a robot come in to give you your medicine, tidy your blankets, and hand you your television remote. Does that sound impossible? It may not be! Scientists are working on a new kind of robot that could be used for just that purpose. These robots have sensors that allow them to feel different textures, have a fake covering that feels like skin, and can see and distinguish objects. They can also move around obstacles more gracefully than in the past. These are the robots you may be seeing in the near future.

Robotics is the technology of the design, construction, and use of robots. It has advanced in leaps and bounds over the past few decades. Compared to what is being built now, the first robots were simple and mechanical. Without them, though, the sophisticated models of today would not exist.

The term *robot* entered language before any had even been created. In 1920, the Czech playwright Karel Čapek first used the word in his play *R.U.R.* to refer to mechanized characters that resembled humans, working on an assembly line. Since that time, *robot* has come to mean a machine that can be programmed to complete a series of tasks without the help of a human.

The person who is credited with inventing the first modern robot is George C. Devol. He designed a programmable mechanical arm in the 1950s. The arm, known as Unimate, weighed four thousand pounds. It could perform a series of steps, following the instructions on a magnetic drum. It was first used on a General Motors assembly line in 1961. It lifted and stacked hot metal parts straight from the mold.

In the following decades, Devol's design was improved. Arms were built that were run with minicomputers. Others had sensors that let them assemble small parts. The direct-drive arm was introduced in 1981. It had motors in its joints that meant it could work faster and more accurately. Devol's technology changed the way many industries produced goods.

Meanwhile, scientists were working on another type of robot. They were creating one that could be used for research purposes. These robots needed to be able to perform tasks that were different from the repetitive motions required for the first industrial machines. A breakthrough occurred in the 1960s when the first mobile robot was developed by a team at Stanford Research Institute. This six-foot-tall robot could move around a room, sensing and avoiding obstacles. It had a television camera, a range finder, bumpers, and a wireless video system. It sent data about its environment to a computer, which then sent commands back to it. The robot was very slow, traveling at only 2 meters (about 6.5 feet) per hour, and quite jerky in its movements. This led to the name "Shakey." The success of Shakey demonstrated the potential for using these kinds of robots in places that were difficult for humans to work in, or even in space.

Other mobile designs followed. The robot Genghis, introduced in 1989, weighed only a little over two pounds. It had six legs that could move independently. Genghis was created by the scientists at the Massachusetts Institute of Technology (MIT) as a way to move across the surface of Mars or other planets. It could send data from the sensors on its legs and cope with rough terrain without losing its balance. The 1990s saw the birth of Dante II, a 1,700-pound robot with eight legs. This robot descended into an active volcano in Alaska in 1994, spending several days at the bottom of the crater collecting data. Genghis, Dante II, and others like them paved the way for the development of mobile robots that are used today, such as the Mars Rover.

Robots can go where no humans have gone before and accomplish tasks that people cannot. As amazing as these robots are, even more impressive is the technology that humans developed that led to these artificially intelligent creatures!

130

Source #3

You have found an article that discusses some of the potential problems with robots.

The Trouble with Robots

You walk into a store looking for a specific book you've heard about from a friend. Instead of a friendly bookstore clerk, a robot meets you! It is just as friendly and even more knowledgeable. The robot quickly and efficiently finds the book you were looking for. It also finds several other books that you might like. This scenario sounds like science fiction, but it's not. It's actually happening in a number of stores across the country. In fact, one hardware chain has introduced robots to help customers find the right product. This trend will likely catch on. Some people feel it's a less expensive and more efficient alternative to having human beings available to help customers.

Is there anything wrong with robots doing the work of human beings? Maybe. For one thing, robots are replacing people, taking away valuable jobs. It's not just happening in stores; it's also happening in manufacturing plants, hospitals, and warehouses.

And it may soon happen in schools. Can you imagine what it would be like to have a robot as a teacher? Would that robot be able to help you understand and solve difficult math problems? Would the robot be able to help you read works of literature? And what would happen to human teachers if robots are introduced to the classroom?

Loss of jobs is just one of the possible problems with robot workers. There is another problem, too. If robots continue to evolve as they have been, will they become super-smart—smarter than human beings? If that does happen, will they develop feelings and emotions? Will they use their super-intelligence against humans?

As early as 1965, Raymond Kurzweil, then only 17 years old, demonstrated that a computer could compose music. While this may not seem surprising, what Kurzweil was really demonstrating was that computers could be creative. Creativity was once considered an entirely human activity, and some may even say that creativity is what actually makes us human.

Kurzweil went on to develop an idea called *singularity*, which claims that technology is increasing so quickly and so significantly that it actually has a runaway effect. In other words, if technology continues to develop at the rate that it is today, by the year 2045 super-intelligent machines, including robots, would totally dominate our world.

Name _____ Date _____

There are other theories regarding what might happen with robots in the near future. Many think that large corporations in wealthy countries would be the only source of robots. This would leave poorer countries without the resources they need to be competitive.

Others think that robots could become capable of actually fixing themselves. In other words, robots might build other robots. Then there would be no need for humans to make more.

Other scientists think that a new kind of being—a *cyborg*—will develop that will combine human beings with robots and super-smart computers. Robotic limbs are already being used on human beings. Computerized mechanisms are also being tested that will help paraplegics develop the ability to walk. What will this part-robot/part-human being be like? Will it create a new version of "super-human beings" capable of unusual strength and abilities? Will these cyborgs control what happens in the world—leaving those of lesser strength powerless?

It is possible that robotic principles could be used to reverse the effects of old age, maybe even prolonging life indefinitely. If that were to happen, would Earth's resources be able to support an ever-growing, ever-aging population?

No one can really tell where super-intelligent robots and computers can lead in the future. But because the future is much closer than we think, the potential problems of this kind of technology should be carefully considered and weighed with the benefits.

Name _____ Date _____

1 Source #1 discusses the way scientists are creating human-like robots and how this can benefit society. Source #2 looks at the history of robots and the ways they have benefited human life. Give two examples from each source about how robots have changed our world.

_____

_____

_____

_____

2 Authors write texts to inform, persuade, or entertain. Look at each of the three sources and think about the author's purpose in writing each one. Write the purpose for each source, and then compare and contrast **two** pairs of sources.

_____

_____

_____

_____

3 Which of the following statements are true about robots? Pick **three** options.

Ⓐ Robots were first developed to compose music.

Ⓑ Robots are used as teachers in schools for young children.

Ⓒ Robotic limbs can make life easier for those who are disabled.

Ⓓ Robots have been developed that can give verbal and nonverbal cues.

Ⓔ Robots, such as the Mars Rover, have made some forms of space exploration possible.

133

Name _____ Date _____

Part 2

You will now review your notes and sources, and plan, draft, revise, and edit your writing. You may use your notes and go back to the sources. Now read your assignment and the information about how your writing will be scored; then begin your work

Your Assignment:

Your teacher wants your class to help the robotics team prepare for competition. Your assignment is to write an argumentative essay about whether robots are helpful or harmful to people.

Using more than one source, develop an argument about robots and whether you think they benefit people or are a disadvantage. Choose the most important information from more than one source to support your argument. Then, write an argumentative essay that is several paragraphs long. Be sure to include information on why some people think robots may or may not be more helpful than harmful, and argue against those reasons. Clearly organize your essay and support your argument with details from the sources. Use your own words except when quoting directly from the sources. Be sure to give the source title or number when using details from the sources.

REMEMBER: A well-written argumentative essay

- is clear and focused.
- is well-organized throughout.
- presents strong support with evidence from sources.
- includes facts and details.
- elaborates with specific and effective language.
- demonstrates adequate command of conventions.

Now begin work on your argumentative essay. Manage your time carefully so that you can

1. plan your argumentative essay.
2. write your argumentative essay.
3. revise and edit the final draft of your argumentative essay.

For Part 2, you are being asked to write an argumentative essay that is several paragraphs long. Write your response in the space below.

Remember to check your notes and your prewriting and planning as you write, and then revise and edit your argumentative essay.

Name _____ Date _____

Name _____ Date _____

Name _____ Date _____

_____

_____

_____

_____

_____

_____

_____

_____

_____

_____

_____

_____

_____

_____

_____

_____

_____

_____

_____

_____

_____

_____

_____

_____